주토피아

DISNEY

CONTENTS

교양 있고 세련된 동물의 유토피아! 주토피아!!

동물이 인간처럼 두 발로 걷고 옷을 입고 생활한다면 어떨까요? 주토피아는 이렇게 교양 있고 세련된 온갖 동물이 모여 사는 도시입니다. 동물의 유토피아처럼 보이는 이 도시는 사실 알고 보면 초식동물과 육식동물 사이의 편견과 차별로 가득 차 있지요.

주토피아 최초의 토끼 경찰관 주디 홉스는 세상을 더 나은 곳으로 만들겠다는 큰 꿈을 가지고 있습니다. 하지만 그녀에게 주어진 일은 고작 주차 단속 임무뿐입니다. 경찰 서장 보고는 마지못해 주디에게 실종 동물 사건 하나를 맡깁니다. 하지만 사건 해결을 위해 주디에게 주어진 시간은 단지 48시간뿐! 그리고 이 시간 내에 실종된 동물을 찾지 못하면 주디는 경찰이라는 그녀의 꿈을 포기해야만 합니다. 주디는 주차 단속 임무 중에 알게 된 뻔뻔한 사기꾼 여우 닉 와일드의 도움을 받아 이 사건을 해결하려고 합니다. 그러던 와중 주디와 닉은 이 사건이 단순한 실종 동물 사건이 아니라는 것을 알게 됩니다. 과연 주디와 닉은 실종된 동물을 찾고 그 뒤에 숨겨진 진실을 파헤칠 수 있을까요?

편견과 차별을 뛰어넘은 동물의 우정을 그려낸 〈주토피아〉를 지금 영화로 읽는 영어원서로 읽어 보세요!

한국인을 위한 맞춤형 영어원서!

원서 읽기는 모두가 인정하는 최고의 영어 공부법입니다. 하지만 영어 구사력이 뛰어나지 않은 보통 영어 학습자들에게는 원서 읽기를 선뜻 시작하기가 부담되는 것도 사실입니다.

이 책은 영어 초보자들도 쉽게 원서 읽기를 시작하고, 꾸준한 읽기를 통해 '영어원서 읽기 습관'을 형성할 수 있도록 만들어진 책입니다. 남녀노소 누구나 좋아할 만한 내용의 원서를 기반으로 내용 이해와 영어 실력 향상을 위한 다양한 콘텐츠를 덧붙이고, 리스닝과 낭독 훈련에 활용할 수 있는 오디오북까지 함께 제공하여, 원서를 부담 없이 읽으면서 자연스럽게 영어 실력을 향상시킬 수 있도록 도와줍니다.

특히 이 책은 원서와 워크북을 분권하여 휴대와 학습이 효과적으로 이루어지도록 배려했습니다. 이는 일반 원서에서 찾아볼 수 없는 특장점으로, 워크북과 오디오북을 적절히 활용하면 더욱 쉽고 재미있게 영어 실력을 향상시킬 수 있습니다. ('원서'와 '워크북' 및 '오디오북 MP3 파일' 3종으로 구성된 패키지가 이상 없이 갖추어져 있는지 다시 한번 확인해 보세요!)

이런 분들께 강력 추천합니다!

- 영어원서 읽기를 처음 시작하는 독자
- 쉽고 재미있는 원서를 찾고 있는 영어 학습자
- 영화 『주토피아』를 재미있게 보신 분
- 특목고 입시를 준비하는 초·중학생
- 토익 600~750점, 고등학교 상위권 수준의 영어 학습자

본문 텍스트

내용이 담긴 본문입니다.

원어민이 읽는 일반 원서와 같은 텍스트지만, 암기해야 할 중요 어휘들은 볼드체로 표시되어 있습니다. 이 어휘들은 지금 들고 계신 워크북에 챕터별로 정리되어 있습니다.

학습 심리학 연구 결과에 따르면, 한 단어씩 따로 외우는 단어 암기는 거의 효과가 없다고 합니다. 단어를 제대로 외우기 위해서는 문맥(context) 속에서 단어를 암기해야 하며, 한 단어당 문맥 속에서 15번 이상 마주칠 때 완벽하게 암기할 수 있다고 합니다.

이 책의 본문에서는 중요 어휘를 볼드체로 강조하여, 문맥 속의 단어들을 더 확실히 인지(word cognition in context)하도록 돕고 있습니다. 또한 대부분의 중요 단어들은 다른 챕터에서도 반복해서 등장하기 때문에 이 책을 읽는 것만으로도 자연스럽게 어휘력을 향상시킬 수 있습니다.

또한 본문 하단에는 내용 이해를 돕기 위한 '각주'가 첨가되어 있습니다. 각주는 굳이 암기할 필요는 없지만, 알아 두면 도움이 될 만한 정보를 설명하고 있습니다. 각주를 참고하면 스토리를 더 깊이 있게 이해할 수 있어 원서를 읽는 재미가 배가됩니다.

워크북(Workbook)

Check Your Reading Speed
챕터마다 단어 수가 기록되어 있어, 리딩 속도를 측정할 수 있습니다. 특히 리딩 속도를 중시하는 독자들이 유용하게 사용할 수 있습니다.

Build Your Vocabulary
본문에 볼드 표시되어 있는 단어들이 정리되어 있습니다. 리딩 전·후에 반복해서 보면 원서를 더욱 쉽게 읽을 수 있고, 어휘력도 빠르게 향상될 것입니다.

단어는 〈스펠링 – 빈도 – 발음기호 – 품사 – 한글 뜻 – 영문 뜻〉 순서로 표기되어 있으며 빈도 표시(★)가 많을수록 필수 어휘입니다. 반복해서 등장하는 단어는 빈도 대신 '복습'으로 표기되어 있습니다. 품사는 아래와 같이 표기했습니다.

n. 명사 │ a. 형용사 │ ad. 부사 │ v. 동사
conj. 접속사 │ prep. 전치사 │ int. 감탄사 │ idiom 숙어 및 관용구

Comprehension Quiz
간단한 퀴즈를 통해 읽은 내용에 대한 이해력을 점검해 볼 수 있습니다.

이 책의 활용법

영어원서 읽기, 이렇게 시작해 보세요!

아래와 같이 프리뷰(Preview) → 리딩(Reading) → 리뷰(Review) 세 단계를 거치면서 읽으면, 더욱 효과적으로 영어 실력을 향상할 수 있습니다.

1. 프리뷰(Preview) : 오늘 읽을 내용을 먼저 점검하자!

- 워크북을 통해 오늘 읽을 챕터에 나와 있는 단어들을 쭉 훑어봅니다. 어떤 단어들이 나오는지, 내가 아는 단어와 모르는 단어는 어떤 것들이 있는지 가벼운 마음으로 살펴봅니다.
- 평소처럼 하나하나 쓰면서 암기하려고 하지는 마세요! 익숙하지 않은 단어들을 주의 깊게 보되, 어차피 리딩을 하면서 점차 익숙해질 단어라는 것을 기억하며 빠르게 훑어봅니다.
- 뒤 챕터로 갈수록 '복습'이라고 표시된 단어들이 늘어나는 것을 알 수 있습니다. '복습' 단어인데도 여전히 익숙하지 않다면 더욱 신경을 써서 봐야겠죠? 매일매일 꾸준히 읽는다면, 익숙한 단어들이 점점 많아진다는 것을 몸으로 느낄 수 있습니다.

2. 리딩(Reading) : 내용에 집중하며 빠르게 읽어 나가자!

- 프리뷰를 마친 후 바로 리딩을 시작합니다. 방금 살펴봤던 어휘들을 문장 속에서 다시 만나게 되는데, 이 과정에서 단어의 쓰임새와 어감을 자연스럽게 익히게 됩니다.
- 모르는 단어나 이해되지 않는 문장이 나오더라도 멈추지 말고 전체적인 맥락을 파악하면서 속도감 있게 읽어 나가세요. 이해되지 않는 문장들은 따로 표시를 하되, 일단 넘어가고 계속 읽는 것이 좋습니다. 뒷부분을 읽다 보면 자연히 이해가 되는 경우도 있고, 정 이해가 되지 않는 부분은 리딩을 마친 이후에 따로 리뷰하는 시간을 가지면 됩니다. 문제집을 풀듯이 모든 문장을 분석하면서 원서를 읽는 것이 아니라, 리딩을 할 때는 리딩에만, 리뷰를 할 때는 리뷰에만 집중하는 것이 필요합니다.
- 볼드 처리된 단어의 의미가 궁금하더라도 워크북을 바로 펼치지 마세요. 정 궁금하다면 한 번씩 참고하는 것도 나쁘진 않지만, 워크북과 원서를 번갈아 보면서 읽는 것은 리딩의 흐름을 끊고 단어 하나하나에 집착하는 좋지 않은 리딩 습관을 심어 줄 수 있습니다.

- 같은 맥락에서 번역서를 구해 원서와 동시에 번갈아 보는 것도 좋은 방법이 아닙니다. 한글 번역을 가지고 있다고 해도 일단 영어로 읽을 때는 영어에만 집중하고 어느 정도 분량을 읽은 후에 번역서와 비교하도록 하세요. 처음부터 완벽하게 이해하려고 하는 것보다는 빠른 속도로 2~3회 반복해서 읽는 방식이 실력 향상에 더 도움이 됩니다. 만일 반복해서 읽어도 내용이 전혀 이해되지 않는다면 좀 더 쉬운 책을 골라 실력을 다진 뒤 다시 도전하는 것이 좋습니다.
- 초보자라면 분당 150단어의 리딩 속도를 목표로 잡고 리딩을 합니다. 분당 150단어는 원어민이 말하는 속도로, 영어 학습자들이 리스닝과 스피킹으로 넘어가기 위해 가장 기초적으로 달성해야 하는 단계입니다. 분당 50~80단어 정도의 낮은 리딩 속도를 가지고 있는 경우는 대부분 '잘못된 리딩 습관'을 가지고 있어서 그렇습니다. 이해가 잘 되지 않더라도 분당 150단어까지는 속도감 있게 읽어 나가도록 하세요.

3. 리뷰(Review) : 이해력을 점검하고 꼼꼼하게 다시 살펴보자!

- 해당 챕터의 Comprehension Quiz를 통해 이해력을 점검해 봅니다.
- 오늘 만난 어휘들을 다시 한번 복습합니다. 이때는 읽으면서 중요하다고 생각했던 단어를 연습장에 써 보면서 꼼꼼하게 외우는 것도 좋습니다.
- 이해가 되지 않는다고 표시해 두었던 부분도 주의 깊게 분석해 봅니다. 다시 한번 문장을 꼼꼼히 읽고, 어떤 이유에서 이해가 되지 않았는지 생각해 봅니다. 따로 메모를 남기거나 노트를 작성하는 것도 좋은 방법입니다.
- 원서를 읽고 리뷰하는 시간을 가지는 것은 영어 실력 향상에 많은 도움이 되기는 하지만, 이 과정을 철저히 지키려다가 원서 읽기의 재미를 반감시키는 것은 바람직하지 않습니다. 그럴 때는 차라리 리뷰를 가볍게 하는 것이 좋을 수 있습니다. '내용에 빠져서 재미있게', 문제집에서는 상상도 못할 '많은 양'을 읽으면서, 매일매일 조금씩 꾸준히 실력을 키워 가는 것이 원서를 활용하는 기본적인 방법이며, 영어 공부의 왕도입니다. 문제집 풀듯이 원서 읽기를 시도하고 접근해서는 실패할 수밖에 없습니다.
- 이런 방식으로 원서를 끝까지 다 읽었다면, 다시 반복해서 읽거나 오디오북을 활용하는 등 다양한 방식으로 원서 읽기를 확장해 나갈 수 있습니다. 이에 대한 자세한 안내가 워크북 말미에 실려 있습니다.

CHAPTERS 1 & 2

1. **How was the world divided in the past?**
   A. Mean or nice
   B. Rich or poor
   C. Animal or plant
   D. Predator or prey

2. **Why was Zootopia so important to Judy?**
   A. It was where she had grown up.
   B. It was where her best friends lived.
   C. It was where anyone could be anything.
   D. It was where prey lived without predators.

3. How did Judy's parents want her to change the world?

A. They wanted her to become an actress.

B. They wanted her to become a teacher.

C. They wanted her to become a police officer.

D. They wanted her to become a carrot farmer.

4. Why did Judy kick Gideon in the face?

A. She did it accidentally and felt sorry.

B. Gideon was bullying her and her friends.

C. Gideon tried to steal her costume, and she wanted it back.

D. Gideon said that she would make a terrible police officer.

5. How was Gideon right about one thing that he said about Judy?

A. She didn't know when to quit.

B. She was too small to protect anyone.

C. She was too weak to stop a predator.

D. The world was too crazy to have bunny cops.

CHAPTER 1

Check Your Reading Speed

1분에 몇 단어를 읽는지 리딩 속도를 측정해보세요.

$$\frac{823 \text{ words}}{\text{reading time (} \qquad \text{) sec}} \times 60 = (\qquad) \text{ WPM}$$

Build Your Vocabulary

ancient [éinʃənt] a. 고대의; 아주 오래된
Ancient means belonging to the distant past, especially to the period in history before the end of the Roman Empire.

predator [prédətər] n. 포식자, 포식 동물; 약탈자
A predator is an animal that kills and eats other animals.

echo [ékou] v. (소리가) 울리다, 메아리치다; n. (소리의) 울림, 메아리, 반향
If a sound echoes, it is reflected off a surface and can be heard again after the original sound has stopped.

barn [ba:rn] n. 곳간, 헛간
A barn is a building on a farm in which crops or animal food can be kept.

makeshift [méikʃift] a. 임시변통의, 일시적인; n. 임시 수단, 미봉책
Makeshift things are temporary and usually of poor quality, but they are used because there is nothing better available.

treachery [trétʃəri] n. 배반
Treachery is behavior or an action in which someone betrays their country or betrays a person who trusts them.

bloodlust [blʌ́dlʌ̀st] n. (살인·폭력의) 강한 충동
If you say that someone is driven by a bloodlust, you mean that they are acting in an extremely violent way because their emotions have been aroused by the events around them.

force [fɔːrs] n. 원동력; 영향력; 힘; v. 억지로 ~하다; ~를 강요하다
If you refer to someone or something as a force in a particular type of activity, you mean that they have a strong influence on it.

prey [prei] n. 먹이, 사냥감; 희생자, 피해자
A creature's prey are the creatures that it hunts and eats in order to live.

scare [skεər] v. 무서워하다; 겁주다, 놀라게 하다; n. 불안(감); 놀람; 공포
(scared a. 무서워하는, 겁먹은)
If you are scared of someone or something, you are frightened of them.

uncontrollable [Ànkəntróuləbl] a. 억제할 수 없는, 걷잡을 수 없는
If you describe a feeling or physical action as uncontrollable, you mean that you cannot control it or prevent yourself from feeling or doing it.

maim [meim] v. 불구로 만들다; 쓸모없게 하다
To maim someone means to injure them so badly that part of their body is permanently damaged.

maul [mɔːl] v. (짐승 등이 할퀴어) 상처를 입히다; 난폭하게 다루다; 혹평하다
If you are mauled by an animal, you are violently attacked by it and badly injured.

leap [liːp] v. (leaped/leapt–leaped/leapt) 뛰다, 뛰어오르다; (서둘러) ∼하다;
n. 높이뛰기, 도약; 급증
If you leap somewhere, you move there suddenly and quickly.

crumple [krʌmpl] v. 쓰러지다; 구기다; 구겨지다; (얼굴이) 일그러지다
If someone crumples, they collapse, for example when they have received a shock.

draw out idiom (필요 이상으로) ∼을 길게 끌다 (drawn–out a. 너무 오래 끄는)
You can describe something as drawn-out when it lasts or takes longer than you would like it to.

confuse [kənfjúːz] v. (사람을) 혼란시키다; 혼동하다 (confused a. 혼란스러워하는)
If you are confused, you do not know exactly what is happening or what to do.

monologue [mánəlɔ̀ːg] n. 독백
A monologue is a long speech which is spoken by one person as an entertainment, or as part of an entertainment such as a play.

banner [bǽnər] n. 현수막
A banner is a long strip of cloth with something written on it.

talent [tǽlənt] n. 재주, (타고난) 재능; 재능 있는 사람
Talent is the natural ability to do something well.

stun [stʌn] v. 어리벙벙하게 하다; 깜짝 놀라게 하다; 기절시키다
If you are stunned by something, you are extremely shocked or surprised by it and are therefore unable to speak or do anything.

vicious [víʃəs] a. 잔인한, 포악한; 사나운, 공격적인
A vicious person or a vicious blow is violent and cruel.

meek [miːk] a. 온순한, 온화한
If you describe a person as meek, you think that they are gentle and quiet, and likely to do what other people say.

label [léibəl] v. 라벨을 붙이다, (표에 정보를) 적다; 꼬리표를 붙이다; n. 표, 라벨; 꼬리표
If something is labelled, a label is attached to it giving information about it.

land [lænd] v. (땅에) 떨어지다; (땅·표면에) 내려앉다, 착륙하다; n. 육지, 땅; 지역
When someone or something lands, they come down to the ground after moving through the air or falling.

settle [setl] v. 놓다; 자리 잡다, 정착하다; 해결하다; 진정시키다
If something settles or if you settle it, it sinks slowly down and becomes still.

evolve [iválv] v. 진화하다; (점진적으로) 발달하다
When animals or plants evolve, they gradually change and develop into different forms.

primitive [prímətiv] a. 원시의; 원시 사회의; 초기의
Primitive means belonging to a very early period in the development of an animal or plant.

savage [sǽvidʒ] a. 야만적인, 흉포한; (비판 등이) 맹렬한; n. 포악한 사람; v. 흉포하게 공격하다
Someone or something that is savage is extremely cruel, violent, and uncontrolled.

robe [roub] n. 길고 헐거운 겉옷; 예복, 가운
A robe is a loose piece of clothing which covers all of your body and reaches the ground.

improvisation [impravəzéiʃən] n. 즉석에서 하기; 즉석에서 한 것
(improvisational a. 즉흥의, 즉흥에 의한)
An improvisation is a performance that an actor or musician has not practiced or planned.

burst [bəːrst] v. (burst–burst) 불쑥 움직이다; 터지다, 파열하다; n. (갑자기) 한바탕 ~을 함; 파열
To burst into or out of a place means to enter or leave it suddenly with a lot of energy or force.

harmony [háːrməni] n. 조화, 화합; 화음
If people are living in harmony with each other, they are living together peacefully rather than fighting or arguing.

reveal [rivíːl] v. (비밀 등을) 밝히다; (보이지 않던 것을) 드러내 보이다
To reveal something means to make people aware of it.

friendly [fréndli] a. 상냥한, 다정한; (행동이) 친절한; 우호적인
If someone is friendly, they behave in a pleasant, kind way, and like to be with other people.

youngster [jʌ́ŋstər] n. 청소년, 아이
Young people, especially children, are sometimes referred to as youngsters.

sprinkle [spriŋkl] v. 뿌리다; ~에 섞다; n. 보슬비
If you sprinkle a thing with something such as a liquid or powder, you scatter the liquid or powder over it.

glitter [glítər] n. (장식용) 반짝이; 반짝반짝 하는 빛; v. 반짝반짝 빛나다; (눈이) 번득이다
Glitter consists of tiny shining pieces of metal. It is glued to things for decoration.

mammal [mǽməl] n. 포유동물
Mammals are animals such as humans, dogs, lions, and whales. In general, female mammals give birth to babies rather than laying eggs, and feed their young with milk.

multitudinous [mʌ̀ltətjúːdənəs] a. 무수히 많은, 다수의
If you describe things as multitudinous, you mean that they are very numerous.

cower [káuər] v. (겁을 먹고) 몸을 웅크리다
If you cower, you bend forward and downward because you are very frightened.

herd [həːrd] n. (짐승의) 떼; (한 무리의) 사람들; v. (특정 방향으로) 이동하다; (짐승을) 몰다
A herd is a large group of animals of one kind that live together.

rip [rip] v. (재빨리·거칠게) 떼어 내다, 뜯어 내다; (갑자기) 찢다; n. (길게) 찢어진 곳
If you rip something away, you remove it quickly and forcefully.

astronaut [ǽstrənɔ̀ːt] n. 우주 비행사
An astronaut is a person who is trained for traveling in a spacecraft.

costume [kástjuːm] n. 의상, 복장; 분장
An actor's or performer's costume is the set of clothes they wear while they are performing.

tax [tæks] n. 세금; v. 세금을 부과하다, 과세하다
Tax is an amount of money that you have to pay to the government so that it can pay for public services.

exempt [igzémpt] v. 면제하다; a. 면제되는 (exemption n. (세금) 공제; 면제)
To exempt a person or thing from a particular rule, duty, or obligation means to state officially that they are not bound or affected by it.

actuary [ǽkʧuèri] n. 보험 회계사, 보험수리사
An actuary is a person who is employed by insurance companies to calculate how much they should charge their clients for insurance.

blind [blaind] a. 맹목적인; 눈이 먼; 눈치 채지 못하는; v. 눈이 멀게 하다; 맹목적이 되게 하다
(blindly ad. 맹목적으로, 무턱대고)
If you say that someone does something blindly, you mean that they do it without having enough information, or without thinking about it.

serve [sə:rv] v. (음식을) 제공하다; (상품·서비스를) 제공하다; (어떤 조직·국가 등을 위해) 일하다
When you serve food and drink, you give people food and drink.

almighty [ɔ:lmáiti] a. 엄청난; 전능하신; n. 신
Almighty means very serious or great in extent.

defend [difénd] v. 방어하다, 수비하다; 옹호하다, 변호하다
If you defend someone or something, you take action in order to protect them.

defenseless [difénslis] a. 무방비의; 방어할 수 없는
Defenceless people, animals, places, or things are weak and unable to protect themselves from attack.

uniform [júːnəfɔ̀ːrm] n. 제복, 유니폼
A uniform is a special set of clothes which some people, for example soldiers or the police, wear to work in and which some children wear at school.

officer [ɔ́:fisər] n. 경찰관; 순경; 장교
Members of the police force can be referred to as officers.

nasty [nǽsti] a. 못된, 심술궂은; 끔찍한, 형편없는
If you describe a person or their behavior as nasty, you mean that they behave in an unkind and unpleasant way.

snicker [sníkər] v. 킬킬거리다; 숨죽여 웃다; n. 키득거림
If you snicker, you laugh quietly in a disrespectful way, for example at something rude or embarrassing.

cop [kap] n. 경찰관
A cop is a policeman or policewoman.

onstage [ànstéidʒ] ad. 무대 위에서, 관객 앞에서
When someone such as an actor or musician goes onstage, they go onto the stage in a theater to give a performance.

remark [rimáːrk] n. 발언, 언급; 주목; v. 언급하다, 말하다
If you make a remark about something, you say something about it.

snap [snæp] v. 딱 하고 움직이다; 찰깍 하고 닫히다; (감정 등이) 한 순간에 무너지다; n. 탁 하는 소리
If you snap your fingers, you make a sharp sound by moving your middle finger quickly across your thumb, for example in order to accompany music or to order someone to do something.

backdrop [bǽkdràp] n. (무대의) 배경; (주위) 배경
A backdrop is a large piece of cloth, often with scenery painted on it, that is hung at the back of a stage while a play is being performed.

skyline [skáilain] n. (건물·언덕 등이) 하늘과 맞닿은 윤곽선, 스카이라인
The skyline is the line or shape that is formed where the sky meets buildings or the land.

ancestor [ǽnsestər] n. 조상, 선조
Your ancestors are the people from whom you are descended.

declare [diklέər] v. 선언하다, 공표하다; 분명히 말하다; (소득·과세 물품 등을) 신고하다
If you declare something, you state officially and formally that it exists or is the case.

bow [bau] ① v. (허리를 굽혀) 절하다; (고개를) 숙이다; n. 절, (고개 숙여 하는) 인사 ② n. 활
When you bow to someone, you briefly bend your body toward them as a formal way of greeting them or showing respect.

dutiful [djúːtifəl] a. 의무감에서 하는; 공손한; 순종적인
If you say that someone is dutiful, you mean that they do everything that they are expected to do.

applause [əplɔ́ːz] n. 박수 (갈채)
Applause is the noise made by a group of people clapping their hands to show approval.

include [inklúːd] v. 포함하다; ~을 (~에) 포함시키다
If one thing includes another thing, it has the other thing as one of its parts.

be in full swing idiom 한창 진행 중인, 무르익은
If something is in full swing, it is operating fully and is no longer in its early stages.

booth [buːθ] n. (임시로 만든) 점포; (칸막이를 한) 작은 공간
A booth is a partly closed area or small tent at a fair, exhibition, or similar event.

ride [raid] n. 놀이 기구; (차량·자전거 등을) 타고 달리기; v. (자전거·오토바이 등을) 타다
In a fairground, a ride is a large machine that people ride on for fun.

give up idiom 포기하다; 그만두다; 단념하다
If you give up, you stop trying to do something, usually because it is too difficult.

complacency [kəmpléisnsi] n. 현 상태에 만족함, 안주
Complacency is a feeling of calm satisfaction with your own abilities or situation that prevents you from trying harder.

amen to that idiom 그 말이 맞다
You say 'amen to that,' when you show that you agree strongly with something that someone has just said.

noble [noubl] a. 고귀한, 숭고한; 귀족의
If you say that something is a noble idea, goal, or action, you admire it because it is based on high moral principles.

profession [prəféʃən] n. 직업; 공언, 선언
A profession is a type of job that requires advanced education or training.

spot [spat] v. 발견하다, 찾다, 알아채다; n. (작은) 점; (특정한) 곳
If you spot something or someone, you notice them.

instant [ínstənt] a. 즉각적인; n. 순간, 아주 짧은 동안 (instantly ad. 즉각, 즉시)
You use instant to describe something that happens immediately.

alert [əlɔ́:rt] a. 경계하는, 조심하는; 기민한; v. (위험 등을) 알리다; n. 경계 태세
If you are alert, you are paying full attention to things around you and are able to deal with anything that might happen.

CHAPTER 2

Check Your Reading Speed

1분에 몇 단어를 읽는지 리딩 속도를 측정해보세요.

$$\frac{479 \text{ words}}{\text{reading time (}\qquad\text{) sec}} \times 60 = (\qquad) \text{ WPM}$$

Build Your Vocabulary

bully [búli] v. (약자를) 괴롭히다; 협박하다; n. (약자를) 괴롭히는 사람
If someone bullies you, they use their strength or power to hurt or frighten you.

meek [mi:k] a. 온순한, 온화한
If you describe a person as meek, you think that they are gentle and quiet, and likely to do what other people say.

butt [bʌt] n. 엉덩이; (무기·도구의) 뭉툭한 끝 부분; v. (머리로) 들이받다
(kick one's butt idiom ~을 혼쭐내다)
To kick someone's ass or butt means to fight them and hurt them.

shove [ʃʌv] n. 힘껏 떠밂; v. (거칠게) 밀치다; 아무렇게나 놓다
A shove is a strong push.

smack [smæk] v. 탁 소리가 나게 치다; 세게 부딪치다; n. 강타; 탁 (하는 소리)
If you smack something somewhere, you put it or throw it there so that it makes a loud, sharp noise.

mock [mak] v. 놀리다, 조롱하다; 무시하다; a. 거짓된, 가짜의
If someone mocks you, they show or pretend that they think you are foolish or inferior, for example by saying something funny about you, or by imitating your behavior.

yelp [jelp] v. 새된 소리를 지르다, 비명을 지르다; n. (날카롭게) 외치는 소리, 비명
If a person or dog yelps, they give a sudden short cry, often because of fear or pain.

cut it out idiom 그만둬; 닥쳐!
You can use 'cut it out' for telling someone to stop doing something that you do not like.

costume [kástju:m] n. 의상, 복장; 분장
An actor's or performer's costume is the set of clothes they wear while they are performing.

loser [lúːzər] n. 실패자, 패배자; (경쟁에서) 패자
If you refer to someone as a loser, you have a low opinion of them because you think they are always unsuccessful.

snarl [snaːrl] v. 으르렁거리듯 말하다; 으르렁거리다; n. 으르렁거림
If you snarl something, you say it in a fierce, angry way.

cop [kap] n. 경찰관
A cop is a policeman or policewoman.

stuff [stʌf] v. (재빨리·되는대로) 쑤셔 넣다; 채워 넣다; n. 것, 물건, 물질; 일
If you stuff something somewhere, you push it there quickly and roughly.

watch out idiom 조심해라!
You say 'watch out,' when you warn someone about something dangerous.

dumb [dʌm] a. 멍청한, 바보 같은; 말을 못 하는
If you say that something is dumb, you think that it is silly and annoying.

predator [prédətər] n. 포식자, 포식 동물; 약탈자
A predator is an animal that kills and eats other animals.

prey [prei] n. 먹이, 사냥감; 희생자, 피해자
A creature's prey are the creatures that it hunts and eats in order to live.

instinct [ínstiŋkt] n. 본능; 직감
Instinct is the natural tendency that a person or animal has to behave or react in a particular way.

pronounce [prənáuns] v. 발음하다; 표명하다, 선언하다
To pronounce a word means to say it using particular sounds.

whisper [hwíspər] v. 속삭이다, 소곤거리다; 은밀히 말하다; n. 속삭임, 소곤거리는 소리
When you whisper, you say something very quietly, using your breath rather than your throat, so that only one person can hear you.

pal [pæl] n. 친구; 이봐
Your pals are your friends.

irritate [írətèit] v. 짜증나게 하다, 거슬리다; 자극하다 (irritated a. 짜증이 난)
If something irritates you, it keeps annoying you.

scare [skɛər] v. 겁주다, 놀라게 하다; 무서워하다; n. 불안(감); 놀람, 공포
If something scares you, it frightens or worries you.

thud [θʌd] n. 쿵 (하고 무거운 것이 떨어지는 소리); v. 쿵 치다; 쿵쿵거리다
A thud is a dull sound, such as that which a heavy object makes when it hits something soft.

cruel [kru:əl] a. 잔혹한, 잔인한; 고통스러운, 괴로운 (cruelly ad. 잔인하게, 무자비하게)
Someone who is cruel deliberately causes pain or distress to people or animals.

cower [káuər] v. (겁을 먹고) 몸을 웅크리다
If you cower, you bend forward and downward because you are very frightened.

twitch [twiʧ] v. 씰룩거리다, 경련하다; 홱 잡아채다; n. 씰룩거림, 경련
If something, especially a part of your body, twitches or if you twitch it, it makes a little jumping movement.

mocking [mákiŋ] a. 비웃는, 조롱하는 (mockingly ad. 조롱하듯이)
A mocking expression or mocking behavior indicates that you think someone or something is stupid or inferior.

taunt [tɔ:nt] v. 놀리다, 비웃다, 조롱하다; n. 놀림, 비웃음, 조롱
If someone taunts you, they say unkind or insulting things to you, especially about your weaknesses or failures.

bam [bæm] int. 펑, 쿵 (하고 부딪치는 소리)
Bam is a sudden very loud noise, as that produced when two objects strike against each other with force.

hind [haind] a. 뒤쪽의, 후방의
An animal's hind legs are at the back of its body.

knock [nak] v. 치다, 부딪치다; (문 등을) 두드리다; n. 문 두드리는 소리; 부딪침
(knock down idiom 때려 눕히다)
To knock someone down means to hit or push them so that they fall to the ground or the floor.

spring [spriŋ] v. (sprang–sprung) (갑자기) 뛰어오르다; 홱 움직이다; 튀다; n. 봄; 생기, 활기; 샘
When a person or animal springs, they jump upward or forward suddenly or quickly.

unsheathe [ʌnʃí:ð] v. ~의 덮개를 벗기다; (칼 등을) 칼집에서 뽑다
If you unsheathe something, you draw or pull it out from a sheath or other covering.

claw [klɔ:] n. (동물·새의) 발톱; v. (손톱·발톱으로) 할퀴다
The claws of a bird or animal are the thin, hard, curved nails at the end of its feet.

fist [fist] n. 주먹
Your hand is referred to as your fist when you have bent your fingers in toward the palm in order to hit someone, to make an angry gesture, or to hold something.

slap [slæp] v. (손바닥으로) 철썩 때리다; 털썩 놓다; n. 철썩 때리기, 치기
If you slap someone, you hit them with the palm of your hand.

dig [dig] v. 찌르다; (구멍 등을) 파다; (무엇을 찾기 위해) 뒤지다; n. 쿡 찌르기
If you dig one thing into another or if one thing digs into another, the first thing is pushed hard into the second, or presses hard into it.

bleed [bli:d] v. 피를 흘리다, 출혈하다
When you bleed, you lose blood from your body as a result of injury or illness.

wipe [waip] v. (먼지·물기 등을) 닦다; 지우다; n. (행주·걸레를 써서) 닦기
If you wipe dirt or liquid from something, you remove it, for example by using a cloth or your hand.

cheek [ʧi:k] n. 뺨, 볼
Your cheeks are the sides of your face below your eyes.

glare [glɛər] v. 노려보다; 환하다, 눈부시다; n. 노려봄; 환한 빛, 눈부심
If you glare at someone, you look at them with an angry expression on your face.

wicked [wíkid] a. 아주 좋은; 못된, 사악한; 짓궂은
You use wicked to describe someone or something that is excellent or wonderful.

awesome [ɔ́:səm] a. 기막히게 좋은, 굉장한; 어마어마한, 엄청난
An awesome person or thing is very impressive and often frightening.

exclaim [ikskléim] v. 소리치다, 외치다
If you exclaim, you cry out suddenly in surprise, strong emotion, or pain.

determine [ditə́:rmin] v. ~을 하기로 결정하다; 알아내다, 밝히다
(determination n. 투지; 결정)
Determination is the quality that you show when you have decided to do something and you will not let anything stop you.

CHAPTERS 3 & 4

1. **How did Judy prove her worth during her training with the cadets for the Zootopia Police Academy?**
   A. She used her cuteness to distract the other cadets.
   B. She used her predator repellent against the other cadets.
   C. She used her rabbit skills, including her strong legs and hearing.
   D. She hoped that they would ignore her since she was smaller than most.

2. **How did Judy's parents feel about her going to Zootopia?**
   A. They were both proud and scared.
   B. They were both proud and excited.
   C. They were both confused and angry.
   D. They were both terrified and nervous.

3. **Why did Judy take the fox repellent from her parents?**
   A. Judy hated foxes and wanted to be safe.
   B. Judy took it because they didn't give her a fox Taser.
   C. Judy thought it would make a funny gift for someone.
   D. Judy wanted them to stop talking so that she could leave.

4. **How did Judy find her way in Zootopia?**
   A. She brought a paper map.
   B. She checked her maps app on her phone.
   C. She talked to a stranger on the street.
   D. She called her friend at the police department.

5. **How did Judy feel about her new apartment?**
   A. She loved it because it was above the Zootopia Police Department.
   B. She loved it even though it was dirty and she had crazy neighbors.
   C. She hated it because the walls were greasy and the neighbors were loud.
   D. She hated it because it was too small and far away from the Zootopia Police Department.

Check Your Reading Speed

1분에 몇 단어를 읽는지 리딩 속도를 측정해보세요.

$$\frac{963 \text{ words}}{\text{reading time } (\quad) \text{ sec}} \times 60 = (\quad) \text{ WPM}$$

Build Your Vocabulary

work one's tail off idiom 뼈 빠지게 일하다
If you work your tail off, you work very hard or to the point of exhaustion.

cadet [kədét] n. (경찰·군대의) 간부 후보생
A cadet is a young man or woman who is being trained in the armed services or the police.

strong-willed [strɔ:ŋ-wíld] a. 의지가 강한, 확고한
Someone who is strong-willed has a lot of determination and always tries to do what they want, even though other people may advise them not to.

physical [fízikəl] a. 육체의; 물질의, 물리적인
Physical qualities, actions, or things are connected with a person's body, rather than with their mind.

get through idiom (곤란 등을) 벗어나다, 극복해 나가다
To get through something means to manage to deal with a difficult situation or to stay alive until it is over.

obstacle [ábstəkl] n. 장애물; 장애
An obstacle is an object that makes it difficult for you to go where you want to go, because it is in your way.

simulate [símjulèit] v. 모의 실험하다; ~ 한 체하다, 가장하다 (simulator n. 모의실험 장치)
A simulator is a device which artificially creates the effect of being in conditions of some kind.

mimic [mímik] v. ~을 모방하다; ~처럼 보이다; (남의) 흉내를 내다
If someone or something mimics another person or thing, they try to be like them.

unique [ju:ní:k] a. 유일무이한, 독특한; 특별한
Something that is unique is the only one of its kind.

ZOOTOPIA

ecosystem [ékousistəm] n. (특정 지역의) 생태계
An ecosystem is all the plants and animals that live in a particular area together with the complex relationship that exists between them and their environment.

make up idiom ~을 이루다; (이야기 등을) 만들어 내다
To make up something means to put it together from several different things.

freeze [fri:z] v. 얼다; (두려움 등으로 몸이) 얼어붙다; n. 동결; 한파 (freezing a. 몹시 추운)
If you say that something is freezing or freezing cold, you are emphasizing that it is very cold.

swelter [swéltər] v. 무더위에 시달리다 (sweltering a. 무더운; 더위에 지친)
If you describe the weather as sweltering, you mean that it is extremely hot and makes you feel uncomfortable.

square [skwɛər] n. (시가지의) 한 구획, 가구; 광장; 정사각형; 제곱; a. 정사각형 모양의; 직각의
In a town or city, a square is a flat open place, often in the shape of a square.

scale [skeil] v. (아주 높고 가파른 곳을) 오르다; n. 규모, 범위; 눈금
If you scale something such as a mountain or a wall, you climb up it or over it.

scorching [skɔ́:rʧiŋ] a. 몹시 뜨거운, 타는 듯한; 맹렬한, 신랄한
Scorching or scorching hot weather or temperatures are very hot indeed.

sandstorm [sǽndstɔ:rm] n. (사막의) 모래 폭풍
A sandstorm is a strong wind in a desert area, which carries sand through the air.

drill [dril] n. (군사) 훈련; 반복 연습; 송곳; v. 훈련시키다; (드릴로) 구멍을 뚫다
A drill is repeated training for a group of people, especially soldiers, so that they can do something quickly and efficiently.

instructor [instrʌ́ktər] n. 강사, 교사 (drill instructor n. 훈련 교관)
An instructor is someone who teaches a skill such as driving or skiing.

doubt [daut] v. 확신하지 못하다, 의심하다, 의문을 갖다; n. 의심, 의혹, 의문
If you doubt whether something is true or possible, you believe that it is probably not true or possible.

persistence [pərsístəns] n. 끈기, 고집; 지속성
If you have persistence, you continue to do something even though it is difficult or other people are against it.

perseverance [pə̀:rsəvíərəns] n. 인내(심)
Perseverance is the quality of continuing with something even though it is difficult.

keep up idiom (~의 속도 등을) 따라가다
If you keep up, you work at the necessary speed so that you progress at the same speed as other people.

sail through idiom (시험 등을) 순조롭게 통과하다
If you sail through something, especially a test, you succeed very easily in it.

knock [nak] v. 치다, 부딪치다; (문 등을) 두드리다; n. 문 두드리는 소리; 부딪침
(knock down idiom 때려 눕히다)
To knock someone down means to hit or push them so that they fall to the ground or the floor.

spar [spa:r] v. 스파링하다; 옥신각신하다
If you spar with someone, you box using fairly gentle blows instead of hitting your opponent hard, either when you are training or when you want to test how quickly your opponent reacts.

graduate [grǽdʒuət] v. 졸업하다, 학위를 받다; n. 졸업자 (graduation n. 졸업식; 졸업)
A graduation is a special ceremony at university, college, or school, at which degrees and diplomas are given to students who have successfully completed their studies.

include [inklú:d] v. 포함하다; ~을 (~에) 포함시키다
If one thing includes another thing, it has the other thing as one of its parts.

sport [spɔ:rt] v. 자랑스럽게 보이다; n. 스포츠, 운동
If you sport something, you wear or are decorated with it.

fat lip [fæt líp] n. (얻어 맞아서) 부어오른 입술
If you have a fat lip, you have a swollen mouth or lip, as from a blow.

black eye [blæk ái] n. (맞아서) 멍든 눈
If someone has a black eye, they have a dark-colored bruise around their eye.

mayor [méiər] n. (시·군 등의) 시장
The mayor of a town or city is the person who has been elected to represent it for a fixed period of time or, in some places, to run its government.

podium [póudiəm] n. 연단, 연설대
A podium is a small platform on which someone stands in order to give a lecture or conduct an orchestra.

announce [ənáuns] v. 발표하다, 알리다; 선언하다
If you announce something, you tell people about it publicly or officially.

mammal [mǽməl] n. 포유동물
Mammals are animals such as humans, dogs, lions, and whales. In general, female mammals give birth to babies rather than laying eggs, and feed their young with milk.

initiative [iníʃiətiv] n. 계획; 진취성; 결단력
An initiative is an important act or statement that is intended to solve a problem.

valedictorian [væ` lədiktɔ́:riən] n. 졸업생 대표 (수석 졸업생)
A valedictorian is the student who has the highest marks in their class when they graduate from high school, college, or university, and who gives a speech at their graduation ceremony.

officer [ɔ́:fisər] n. 경찰관; 순경; 장교
Members of the police force can be referred to as officers.

assistant [əsístənt] a. 부(副)-, 조(助)-, 보조의; n. 조수, 보조원
Assistant is used in front of titles or jobs to indicate a slightly lower rank.

badge [bædʒ] n. (경찰 등의) 신분증; 표, 배지
A badge is a piece of metal or cloth which you wear to show that you belong to an organization or support a cause.

privilege [prívəlidʒ] n. 영광; 특권; 특전; v. 특권을 주다
You can use privilege in expressions such as be a privilege or have the privilege when you want to show your appreciation of someone or something or to show your respect.

assign [əsáin] v. (사람을) 배치하다; (일·책임 등을) 맡기다; ~의 탓으로 하다
If someone is assigned to a particular place, group, or person, they are sent there, usually in order to work at that place or for that person.

precinct [prí:siŋkt] n. (경찰) 관할구; 관할 경찰서; 구역, 지구
A precinct is a part of a city which has its own police force and fire service.

deafening [défəniŋ] a. 귀청이 터질 듯한, 귀가 먹먹한
A deafening noise is a very loud noise.

applause [əplɔ́:z] n. 박수 (갈채)
Applause is the noise made by a group of people clapping their hands to show approval.

sob [sab] v. (흑흑) 흐느끼다, 흐느껴 울다; n. 흐느껴 울기, 흐느낌
When someone sobs, they cry in a noisy way, breathing in short breaths.

diploma [diplóumə] n. 졸업장; 수료증
A diploma is a qualification which may be awarded to a student by a university or college, or by a high school in the United States.

pin [pin] v. (핀으로) 고정시키다; 꼼짝 못하게 하다; n. 핀
If you pin something on or to something, you attach it with a pin, a drawing pin, or a safety pin.

uniform [júːnəfɔ̀ːrm] n. 제복, 유니폼
A uniform is a special set of clothes which some people, for example soldiers or the police, wear to work in and which some children wear at school.

congratulation [kəngræʧuléiʃən] n. (pl.) 축하해요!; 축하
You can use 'congratulations' for telling someone that you are pleased about their success, good luck, or happiness on a special occasion.

let down idiom ~의 기대를 저버리다, ~를 실망시키다
If you let someone down, you disappoint them by failing to do what you agreed to do or were expected to do.

whisper [hwíspər] v. 속삭이다, 소곤거리다; 은밀히 말하다; n. 속삭임, 소곤거리는 소리
When you whisper, you say something very quietly, using your breath rather than your throat, so that only one person can hear you.

make room idiom 공간을 만들다; 자리를 내다; 길을 양보하다
If you make room, you move aside or move something aside to allow someone to enter or pass or to clear space for something.

edge [edʒ] v. 조금씩 움직이다; 테두리를 두르다; n. 끝, 가장자리; 우위
If someone or something edges somewhere, they move very slowly in that direction.

sibling [síbliŋ] n. 형제, 자매
Your siblings are your brothers and sisters.

accompany [əkʌ́mpəni] v. 동반하다, 동행하다; 수반하다
If you accompany someone, you go somewhere with them.

thrill [θril] v. 열광시키다, 정말 신나게 하다; n. 흥분, 설렘; 전율 (thrilled a. 아주 흥분한, 신이 난)
If someone is thrilled, they are extremely pleased about something.

terrify [térəfài] v. (몹시) 무섭게 하다 (terrified a. (몹시) 무서워하는, 겁이 난)
If something terrifies you, it makes you feel extremely frightened.

to say nothing of idiom (게다가) ~은 말할 것도 없고
You use to say nothing of when you mention an additional thing which gives even more strength to the point you are making.

★ **perplex** [pərpléks] v. 당혹하게 하다 (perplexed a. 당혹한, 당혹스러운)
If you are perplexed, you feel confused and slightly worried by something because you do not understand it.

⁂ **cheat** [tʃiːt] v. 부정행위를 하다; 속이다, 사기 치다; n. 사기꾼; 속임수
When someone cheats, they do not obey a set of rules which they should be obeying, for example in a game or exam.

★ **biology** [baiálədʒi] n. 생태; 생물학
The biology of a living thing is the way in which its body or cells behave.

★ **jerk** [dʒəːrk] n. 얼간이; 홱 움직임; v. 홱 움직이다
If you call someone a jerk, you are insulting them because you think they are stupid or you do not like them.

in case idiom (~할) 경우에 대비해서
If you do something in case or just in case a particular thing happens, you do it because that thing might happen.

care package [kéər pækidʒ] n. (가족에게 보내는) 일용품 꾸러미
A care package is a package of useful or enjoyable items that is sent or given as a gift to someone who is away from home.

★ **bunch** [bʌntʃ] n. (양·수가) 많음; 다발, 묶음
A bunch of things is a number of things, especially a large number.

★ **spray** [sprei] n. 분무기, 스프레이; 뿌리기; v. (분무기로) 뿌리다; (아주 많이) 퍼붓다
A spray is a liquid kept under pressure in a can or other container, which you can force out in very small drops.

canister [kǽnəstər] n. 금속 용기; 작은 깡통
A canister is a strong metal container. It is used to hold gases or chemical substances.

repellent [ripélənt] n. 방충제; a. 역겨운, 혐오감을 주는
Insect repellent is a product containing chemicals that you spray into the air or on your body in order to keep insects away.

deterrent [ditə́ːrənt] n. 제지하는 것
A deterrent is a weapon or set of weapons designed to prevent enemies from attacking by making them afraid to do so.

horn [hɔːrn] n. (차량의) 경적; (양·소 등의) 뿔
On a vehicle such as a car, the horn is the device that makes a loud noise as a signal or warning.

go overboard idiom 잔뜩 흥분하다
If you say that someone goes overboard, you mean that they do something to a greater extent than is necessary or reasonable.

check out idiom (흥미로운 것을) 살펴보다; ~을 확인하다
If you check someone or something out, you look at or examine a person or thing that seems interesting or attractive.

sizzle [sizl] v. 지글지글 하는 소리를 내다
If something such as hot oil or fat sizzles, it makes hissing sounds.

goodness [gúdnis] int. 와!, 어머나!, 맙소사!; n. 신; 선량함
People sometimes say 'goodness' or 'my goodness' to express surprise.

sake [seik] n. 목적; 원인, 이유 (for goodness' sake idiom 제발, 부디, 맙소사)
Some people use expressions such as 'for God's sake,' 'for heaven's sake,' or 'for goodness' sake' in order to express annoyance or impatience, or to add force to a question or request.

grab [græb] v. (와락·단단히) 붙잡다; 급히 ~하다; n. 와락 잡아채려고 함
If you grab something, you take it or pick it up suddenly and roughly.

terrific [tərífik] a. 아주 좋은, 멋진, 훌륭한; (양·정도 등이) 엄청난
If you describe something or someone as terrific, you are very pleased with them or very impressed by them.

exclaim [ikskléim] v. 소리치다, 외치다
If you exclaim, you cry out suddenly in surprise, strong emotion, or pain.

conductor [kəndʌ́ktər] n. (버스나 기차의) 안내원; 지휘자
On a train, a conductor is a person whose job is to travel on the train in order to help passengers and check tickets.

hold back idiom (감정을) 누르다; ~을 저지하다; (진전·발전을) 저해하다
If you hold back something, you stop yourself from expressing or showing how you feel.

wrap [ræp] v. (무엇의 둘레를) 두르다; 포장하다; 둘러싸다; n. 포장지; 랩
If someone wraps their arms, fingers, or legs around something, they put them firmly around it.

waterworks [wɔ́ːtərwəːrks] n. 눈물; 수도, 급수 시설
Waterworks can refer to the shedding of tears.

flow [flou] v. (액체·기체가) 흐르다; (많은 사람들·사물들이) 계속 이동하다; n. 흐름
If a liquid, gas, or electrical current flows somewhere, it moves there steadily and continuously.

pull together idiom 정신 차리다; 가라앉다; 함께 일하다, 협력하다
If you pull it together or pull yourself together, you gain control of your feelings and start to act in a calm and sensible way.

pull away idiom (차량이) 움직이기 시작하다
When a vehicle pulls away, it begins to move.

wave [weiv] v. (손·팔을) 흔들다; 흔들리다; 손짓하다; n. 파도, 물결; (팔·손·몸을) 흔들기
If you wave or wave your hand, you move your hand from side to side in the air, usually in order to say hello or goodbye to someone.

fade [feid] v. 서서히 사라지다, 점점 희미해지다; 바래다, 희미해지다
When something that you are looking at fades, it slowly becomes less bright or clear until it disappears.

distance [dístəns] n. 먼 곳; 거리; v. (~에) 관여하지 않다 (into the distance idiom 저 먼 곳에)
If you can see something into the distance, you can see it, far away from you.

observation [àbzərvéiʃən] n. 관찰, 관측; 의견 (observation deck n. 전망대)
Observation is the action or process of carefully watching someone or something.

deck [dek] n. (배의) 갑판; 층; v. 꾸미다, 장식하다
A deck on a vehicle such as a bus or ship is a lower or upper area of it.

click [klik] v. (마우스를) 클릭하다; 딸깍 하는 소리를 내다; n. 찰칵 (하는 소리); (마우스를) 클릭함
If you click on an area of a computer screen, you point the cursor at that area and press one of the buttons on the mouse in order to make something happen.

CHAPTER 4

Check Your Reading Speed

1분에 몇 단어를 읽는지 리딩 속도를 측정해보세요.

$$\frac{269 \text{ words}}{\text{reading time (}\quad\text{) sec}} \times 60 = (\quad) \text{ WPM}$$

Build Your Vocabulary

bend [bend] n. (도로 · 강의) 굽이, 굽은 곳; v. (몸 · 머리를) 굽히다, 숙이다; 구부리다
A bend in a road, pipe, or other long thin object is a curve or angle in it.

gaze [geiz] v. (가만히) 응시하다, 바라보다; n. 응시, (눈여겨보는) 시선
If you gaze at someone or something, you look steadily at them for a long time.

incredible [inkrédəbl] a. 믿을 수 없는, 믿기 힘든
If you describe something or someone as incredible, you like them very much or are impressed by them, because they are extremely or unusually good.

sight [sait] n. 광경, 모습; 시야; 보기, 봄; v. 갑자기 보다
A sight is something that you see.

distance [dístəns] n. 먼 곳; 거리; v. (~에) 관여하지 않다 (in the distance idiom 저 먼 곳에)
If you can see something in the distance, you can see it, far away from you.

press [pres] v. (무엇에) 바짝 대다; 누르다; 꾹 밀어 넣다; n. 언론; 인쇄
If you press something somewhere, you push it firmly against something else.

borough [bɔ́:rou] n. 자치구
A borough is a town, or a district within a large town, which has its own council.

serve [sə:rv] v. (상품 · 서비스를) 제공하다; (음식을) 제공하다; (어떤 조직 · 국가 등을 위해) 일하다
If something serves people or an area, it provides them with something that they need.

downtown [dauntáun] n. 도심지; 상업 지구; ad. 시내에
Downtown places are in or toward the center of a large town or city, where the shops and places of business are.

make one's way idiom 나아가다, 가다
When you make your way somewhere, you walk or travel there.

earbud [íərbʌd] n. (pl.) 이어폰
Earbuds are very small headphones that you wear in your ears.

chaotic [keiátik] a. 혼돈 상태인
Something that is chaotic is in a state of complete disorder and confusion.

wash over idiom (감정·느낌이) 밀려오다
If a feeling washes over you, you suddenly feel it very strongly and cannot control it.

awestruck [ɔ́:strʌk] a. 경이로워하는
If someone is awestruck, they are very impressed and amazed by something.

‡ **rush** [rʌʃ] v. 급(속)히 움직이다; 서두르다; 재촉하다; n. 혼잡, 분주함
If you rush somewhere, you go there quickly.

be a far cry from idiom ~와는 크게 다르다
Something that is a far cry from something else is very different from it.

figure out idiom ~을 이해하다, 알아내다; 계산하다, 산출하다
If you figure out someone or something, you come to understand them by thinking carefully.

* **landlady** [lǽndlèidi] n. (집·방 등의) 여자 주인
Someone's landlady is the woman who allows them to live or work in a building which she owns, in return for rent.

let in idiom ~을 들어오게 하다
If you let someone or something in, you allow them to enter a room or a building.

complimentary [kàmpləméntəri] a. 무료의; 칭찬하는
A complimentary seat, ticket, or book is given to you free.

delouse [di:láus] v. 이를 없애다
To delouse means to rid a person or animal of lice as a sanitary measure.

‡ **neighbor** [néibər] n. 이웃 (사람); v. 이웃하다, 인접하다
Your neighbor is someone who lives near you.

hallway [hɔ́:lwèi] n. 복도; 통로; 현관
A hallway in a building is a long passage with doors into rooms on both sides of it.

‡ **greet** [gri:t] v. 인사하다; 환영하다; 반응을 보이다
When you greet someone, you say 'Hello' or shake hands with them.

apologize [əpálədʒàiz] v. 사과하다
When you apologize to someone, you say that you are sorry that you have hurt them or caused trouble for them.

slam [slæm] v. 쾅 닫다; 세게 밀다; n. 쾅 하고 닫기; 탕 하는 소리
If you slam a door or window or if it slams, it shuts noisily and with great force.

greasy [grí:si] a. 기름투성이의, 기름이 많이 묻은
Something that is greasy has a thick, oily substance on it or in it.

rickety [ríkiti] a. 곧 무너질 듯한; 낡아빠진, 황폐한
A rickety structure or piece of furniture is not very strong or well made, and seems likely to collapse or break.

flop [flap] v. 털썩 주저앉다; ~을 떨어뜨리다; 퍼덕거리다; n. 실패작
If you flop into a chair, for example, you sit down suddenly and heavily because you are so tired.

CHAPTERS 5 & 6

1. **Why did Clawhauser apologize to Judy when they first met?**
   A. Clawhauser had called her "cute."
   B. Clawhauser was eating with his mouth open.
   C. Clawhauser had eaten the last donut without sharing.
   D. Clawhauser had trouble hearing her because she was small.

2. **How did Chief Bogo feel about the new recruits?**
   A. He was excited to have new people help out.
   B. He didn't care about even introducing them.
   C. He was upset that he had more work to do now.
   D. He was nervous about them causing more problems for him.

3. **What was the first priority for the Zootopia Police Department?**
   A. Missing mammal cases
   B. Missing donut cases
   C. Parking duty
   D. Parade duty

4. **Why did Judy feel bad about being suspicious of the fox at the ice cream parlor?**
   A. The fox was just trying to get ice cream with his son.
   B. The fox was sneaking around trying to steal ice cream.
   C. The fox noticed that Judy had fox repellent in her hand.
   D. The fox was looking for a fox ice cream parlor but was just lost.

5. **How did Judy help the fox dad and son?**
   A. She got the elephant to apologize to the dad and son.
   B. She got the elephant to give them free ice cream since it was the boy's birthday.
   C. She got the elephant to sell ice cream to them and even paid for it herself.
   D. She got the elephant to give them directions to the nearest fox ice cream parlor.

CHAPTER 5

Check Your Reading Speed

1분에 몇 단어를 읽는지 리딩 속도를 측정해보세요.

$$\frac{803 \text{ words}}{\text{reading time ( ) sec}} \times 60 = (\quad) \text{ WPM}$$

Build Your Vocabulary

beep [bi:p] n. 삑 (하는 소리); v. 삐 소리를 내다; (경적을) 울리다
A beep is a short, loud sound like that made by a car horn or a telephone answering machine.

alarm [əlá:rm] n. 자명종; 경보 장치; 불안, 공포; v. 불안하게 하다; 경보장치를 달다
An alarm is the same as an alarm clock which is a clock that you can set to make a noise so that it wakes you up at a particular time.

spring [spriŋ] v. (sprang–sprung) (갑자기) 뛰어오르다; 휙 움직이다; 튀다; n. 봄; 생기, 활기; 샘
When a person or animal springs, they jump upward or forward suddenly or quickly.

rinse [rins] v. 씻어 내다; 헹구다; n. (물에) 씻기, 헹구기
When you rinse something, you wash it in clean water in order to remove dirt or soap from it.

vest [vest] n. 조끼
A vest is a sleeveless piece of clothing with buttons which people usually wear over a shirt.

pin [pin] v. (핀으로) 고정시키다; 꼼짝 못하게 하다; n. 핀
If you pin something on or to something, you attach it with a pin, a drawing pin, or a safety pin.

badge [bædʒ] n. (경찰 등의) 신분증; 표, 배지
A badge is a piece of metal or cloth which you wear to show that you belong to an organization or support a cause.

strap [stræp] v. 끈으로 묶다; 붕대를 감다; n. 끈, 줄, 띠
If you strap something somewhere, you fasten it there with a strap.

glance [glæns] v. 흘깃 보다; 대충 훑어보다; n. 흘깃 봄
If you glance at something or someone, you look at them very quickly and then look away again immediately.

repellent [ripélənt] n. 방충제; a. 역겨운, 혐오감을 주는
Insect repellent is a product containing chemicals that you spray into the air or on your body in order to keep insects away.

grab [græb] v. (와락·단단히) 붙잡다; 급히 ～하다; n. 와락 잡아채려고 함
If you grab something, you take it or pick it up suddenly and roughly.

in case idiom (～할) 경우에 대비해서
If you do something in case or just in case a particular thing happens, you do it because that thing might happen.

widen [waidn] v. 넓어지다; (정도·범위 등이) 커지다
If your eyes widen, they open more.

chaotic [keiátik] a. 혼돈 상태인
Something that is chaotic is in a state of complete disorder and confusion.

burly [bə́:rli] a. 건장한, 억센
A burly man has a broad body and strong muscles.

criminal [krímənl] n. 범인, 범죄자; a. 범죄의; 형사상의
A criminal is a person who regularly commits crimes.

rush [rʌʃ] v. 급(속)히 움직이다; 서두르다; 재촉하다; n. 혼잡, 분주함
If you rush somewhere, you go there quickly.

dodge [dadʒ] v. (몸을) 재빨리 움직이다; 기피하다; n. 몸을 홱 피함
If you dodge something, you avoid it by quickly moving aside or out of reach so that it cannot hit or reach you.

husky [hʌ́ski] a. 건장한, 튼튼한; (목소리가) 약간 쉰 듯한
If you describe a man as husky, you think that he is tall, strong, and attractive.

pudgy [pʌ́dʒi] a. 땅딸막한, 통통한
If you describe someone as pudgy, you mean that they are rather fat in an unattractive way.

friendly [fréndli] a. 상냥한, 다정한; (행동이) 친절한; 우호적인
If someone is friendly, they behave in a pleasant, kind way, and like to be with other people.

* **chat** [ʧæt] v. 이야기를 나누다, 수다를 떨다; n. 이야기, 대화
When people chat, they talk to each other in an informal and friendly way.

: **lean** [li:n] v. 기울이다, (몸을) 숙이다; ~에 기대다; a. 군살이 없는, 호리호리한
When you lean in a particular direction, you bend your body in that direction.

goodness [gúdnis] int. 와!, 어머나!, 맙소사!; n. 신; 선량함
People sometimes say 'goodness' or 'my goodness' to express surprise.

* **hire** [haiər] v. (사람을) 고용하다; 빌리다
If you hire someone, you employ them or pay them to do a particular job for you.

wince [wins] v. (통증·당혹감으로) 움찔하고 놀라다
If you wince, the muscles of your face tighten suddenly because you have felt a pain or because you have just seen, heard, or remembered something unpleasant.

flabby [flǽbi] a. (군살이) 축 늘어진; 무기력한, 힘없는
Flabby people are rather fat, with loose flesh over their bodies.

stereotype [stériətàip] v. 고정 관념을 형성하다, 정형화하다; n. 고정 관념
If someone is stereotyped as something, people form a fixed general idea or image of them, so that it is assumed that they will behave in a particular way.

apologetic [əpàlədʒétik] a. 미안해하는, 사과하는 (apologetically ad. 변명하여)
If you are apologetic, you show or say that you are sorry for causing trouble for someone, for hurting them, or for disappointing them.

* **stammer** [stǽmər] v. 말을 더듬다; n. 말 더듬기
If you stammer, you speak with difficulty, hesitating and repeating words or sounds.

figure out idiom ~을 이해하다, 알아내다; 계산하다, 산출하다
If you figure out someone or something, you come to understand them by thinking carefully.

fold [fould] n. 주름; 접힌 부분; v. 접다; (두 손·팔 등을) 끼다
A fold is an area of skin that sags or hangs loosely.

* **joyful** [dʒɔ́ifəl] a. 아주 기뻐하는; 기쁜 (joyfully ad. 기쁘게)
Someone who is joyful is extremely happy.

* **cram** [kræm] v. (억지로) 밀어 넣다
If you cram things or people into a container or place, you put them into it, although there is hardly enough room for them.

roll call [róul kɔ̀:l] n. 점호, 출석조사
If you take a roll call, you check which of the members of a group are present by reading their names out.

. **tower** [táuər] v. (~보다) 매우 높다; 솟다; n. 탑
Someone or something that towers over surrounding people or things is a lot taller than they are.

. **massive** [mǽsiv] a. (육중하면서) 거대한; 엄청나게 심각한
Something that is massive is very large in size, quantity, or extent.

복습 **gaze** [geiz] v. (가만히) 응시하다, 바라보다; n. 응시, (눈여겨보는) 시선
If you gaze at someone or something, you look steadily at them for a long time.

복습 **extend** [iksténd] v. (팔·다리를) 뻗다; 더 길게 만들다; 연장하다
If someone extends their hand, they stretch out their arm and hand to shake hands with someone.

. **paw** [pɔ:] n. (동물의) 발; v. 발로 긁다; (함부로) 건드리다
The paws of an animal such as a cat, dog, or bear are its feet, which have claws for gripping things and soft pads for walking on.

. **gigantic** [dʒaigǽntik] a. 거대한
If you describe something as gigantic, you are emphasizing that it is extremely large in size, amount, or degree.

. **tag** [tæg] n. 꼬리표; v. 꼬리표를 붙이다 (name tag n. 명찰)
A tag is a small piece of card or cloth which is attached to an object or person and has information about that object or person on it.

복습 **sincere** [sinsíər] a. 진실된, 진정한, 진심 어린; 진심의 (sincerely ad. 진심으로)
If you say or feel something sincerely, you really mean or feel it, and are not pretending.

. **snort** [snɔ:rt] v. 코웃음을 치다, 콧방귀를 뀌다; n. 코웃음, 콧방귀
If someone snorts something, they say it in a way that shows contempt.

. **reluctant** [rilʌ́ktənt] a. 꺼리는, 마지못한, 주저하는 (reluctantly ad. 마지못해, 꺼려하여)
If you are reluctant to do something, you are unwilling to do it and hesitate before doing it, or do it slowly and without enthusiasm.

복습 **fist** [fist] n. 주먹
Your hand is referred to as your fist when you have bent your fingers in toward the palm in order to hit someone, to make an angry gesture, or to hold something.

bump [bʌmp] n. 부딪치기, 충돌; 쿵, 탁 (하고 부딪치는 소리); v. (~에) 부딪치다; 덜컹거리며 가다
A bump is the action or the dull sound of two heavy objects hitting each other.

chief [ʧi:f] n. (단체의) 최고위자; 추장, 족장; a. 주된; (계급·직급상) 최고위자인
The chief of an organization is the person who is in charge of it.

gruff [grʌf] a. (행동이) 거친; (목소리가) 걸걸한
If you describe someone as gruff, you mean that they seem rather unfriendly or bad-tempered.

instant [ínstənt] a. 즉각적인; n. 순간, 아주 짧은 동안 (instantly ad. 즉각, 즉시)
You use instant to describe something that happens immediately.

fall in line idiom 규정에 따르다, 협조하다
If a person in an organization falls in line, they start to follow the rules and behave according to expected standards of behavior.

stomp [stamp] v. 쿵쿵거리며 걷다, 발을 구르다; 짓밟다
If you stomp somewhere, you walk there with very heavy steps, often because you are angry.

docket [dákit] n. (회의 등의) 협의 사항; 명세서; 사건 일람표
A docket is a list of business to be discussed or things to be done, especially at a meeting.

acknowledge [æknálidʒ] v. 알은 척하다, 안다는 표시를 보이다; 인정하다
If you acknowledge someone, for example by moving your head or smiling, you show that you have seen and recognized them.

nod [nad] v. (고개를) 끄덕이다, 까딱하다; n. (고개를) 끄덕임
If you nod in a particular direction, you bend your head once in that direction in order to indicate something or to give someone a signal.

blush [blʌʃ] v. 얼굴을 붉히다; ~에 부끄러워하다; n. 얼굴이 붉어짐
When you blush, your face becomes redder than usual because you are ashamed or embarrassed.

clap [klæp] v. 박수를 치다; (갑자기·재빨리) 놓다; n. 박수; 쿵 하는 소리
When you clap, you hit your hands together to show appreciation or attract attention.

hoot [hu:t] v. 시끄럽게 떠들어대다; 폭소를 터뜨리다; 콧방귀를 뀌다; n. 폭소; 비웃음
If you hoot, you make a loud high-pitched noise when you are laughing or showing disapproval.

recruit [rikrú:t] n. 신임 경찰; 신병; 새로운 구성원; v. 모집하다; (남을) 설득하다
A recruit is a person who has recently joined an organization or an army.

gesture [dʒéstʃər] v. (손·머리 등으로) 가리키다; 몸짓을 하다; n. 몸짓; (감정·의도의) 표시
If you gesture, you use movements of your hands or head in order to tell someone something or draw their attention to something.

pushpin [púʃpìn] n. 제도용 압정
A pushpin is a pin with a small ball-shaped head, used to fasten papers to a bulletin board or to indicate positions on charts and maps.

tail [teil] n. (동물의) 꼬리; 끝부분; v. 미행하다
The tail of an animal, bird, or fish is the part extending beyond the end of its body.

priority [praió:rəti] n. 우선 사항; 우선, 우선권
If something is a priority, it is the most important thing you have to do or deal with, or must be done or dealt with before everything else you have to do.

assign [əsáin] v. (일·책임 등을) 맡기다; (사람을) 배치하다; ~의 탓으로 하다
(assignment n. 과제, 임무)
An assignment is a task or piece of work that you are given to do, especially as part of your job or studies.

bark [ba:rk] v. (명령·질문 등을) 빽 내지르다; (개가) 짖다; n. (개 등이) 짖는 소리; 나무껍질
If you bark at someone, you shout at them aggressively in a loud, rough voice.

district [dístrikt] n. 지구, 지역, 구역
A district is a particular area of a town or country.

square [skwɛər] n. (시가지의) 한 구획, 가구; 광장; 정사각형; 제곱; a. 정사각형 모양의; 직각의
In a town or city, a square is a flat open place, often in the shape of a square.

anxious [ǽŋkʃəs] a. 간절히 바라는; 불안해하는, 염려하는 (anxiously ad. 간절히; 걱정스럽게)
If you are anxious to do something or anxious that something should happen, you very much want to do it or very much want it to happen.

dramatic [drəmǽtik] a. 과장된; 극적인; 감격적인, 인상적인 (dramatically ad. 극적으로)
A dramatic action, event, or situation is exciting and impressive.

dismiss [dismís] v. (사람을) 해산시키다; 묵살하다; (생각·느낌을) 떨쳐 버리다
If you are dismissed by someone in authority, they tell you that you can go away from them.

ankle [ǽŋkl] n. 발목

Your ankle is the joint where your foot joins your leg.

token [tóukən] a. 형식적인, 시늉에 불과한; n. 선물권; 표시, 징표

You use token to refer to something that is done to prevent other people complaining, although it is not sincerely meant and has no real effect.

slam [slæm] v. 쾅 닫다; 세게 밀다; n. 쾅 하고 닫기; 탕 하는 소리

If you slam a door or window or if it slams, it shuts noisily and with great force.

Check Your Reading Speed

1분에 몇 단어를 읽는지 리딩 속도를 측정해보세요.

$$\frac{955 \text{ words}}{\text{reading time (} \quad \text{) sec}} \times 60 = (\quad) \text{ WPM}$$

Build Your Vocabulary

sport [spɔːrt] v. 자랑스럽게 보이다; n. 스포츠, 운동
If you sport something, you wear or are decorated with it.

traffic [træfik] n. 차량들, 교통(량); 운항, 운행; 수송
Traffic refers to all the vehicles that are moving along the roads in a particular area.

enforcement [infɔ́ːrsmənt] n. (법률의) 시행, 집행; 강제
If someone carries out the enforcement of an act or rule, they make sure that it is obeyed, usually by punishing people who do not obey it.

vest [vest] n. 조끼
A vest is a sleeveless piece of clothing with buttons which people usually wear over a shirt.

buckle [bʌkl] v. 버클로 잠그다; 찌그러지다; 휘어지다; n. 버클, 잠금장치
(buckle up idiom 버클을 채우다)
If you buckle up, you fasten the belt that you wear in a vehicle to keep you in your seat if there is an accident.

shade [ʃeid] n. (pl.) 선글라스; 그늘; 약간, 기미; v. 그늘지게 하다
Shades are sunglasses.

press [pres] v. 누르다; (무엇에) 바짝 내다; 쑥 밀어 넣다; n. 언론; 인쇄
If you press something or press down on it, you push hard against it with your foot or hand.

take off idiom (서둘러) 떠나다; 날아오르다
If you take off, you leave somewhere suddenly or in a hurry.

twist [twist] v. (고개·몸 등을) 돌리다; 구부리다; (도로·강이) 구불구불하다;
n. (고개·몸 등을) 돌리기
If you twist part of your body such as your head or your shoulders, you turn that part while keeping the rest of your body still.

expire [ikspáiər] v. (기한이) 만료되다, 만기가 되다 (expired a. 만료된, 기한이 지난)
When something such as a contract, deadline, or visa expires, it comes to an end or is no longer valid.

ding [diŋ] v. 딩동 하는 소리를 내다; (차체 등을) 쿵 들이받다; n. 딩동, 땡 (하는 소리)
If something dings, it makes a ringing sound.

dash [dæʃ] v. (급히) 서둘러 가다; 내동댕이치다; n. 돌진, 질주; 단거리 경주
If you dash somewhere, you run or go there quickly and suddenly.

dozen [dʌzn] n. (pl.) 다수, 여러 개; 12개; 십여 개
If you refer to dozens of things or people, you are emphasizing that there are very many of them.

boom [buːm] n. 쾅 (하는 소리); v. 쾅 하는 소리를 내다; 굵은 목소리로 말하다
Boom can refer to a sudden loud noise, often used to indicate a sudden impact or occurrence.

self-satisfied [sèlf-sǽtisfàid] a. 자기만족에 빠진, 자기만족적인
If you describe someone as self-satisfied, you mean that they are too pleased with themselves about their achievements or their situation and they think that nothing better is possible.

horn [hɔːrn] n. (차량의) 경적; (양·소 등의) 뿔
On a vehicle such as a car, the horn is the device that makes a loud noise as a signal or warning.

yell [jel] v. 고함치다, 소리 지르다; n. 고함, 외침
If you yell, you shout loudly, usually because you are excited, angry, or in pain.

interrupt [ìntərʌ́pt] v. (말·행동을) 방해하다; 중단시키다; 차단하다
If you interrupt someone who is speaking, you say or do something that causes them to stop.

suspicious [səspíʃəs] a. 의혹을 갖는, 수상쩍어 하는; 의심스러운
(suspiciously ad. 수상쩍게; 미심쩍다는 듯이)
If you are suspicious of someone or something, you believe that they are probably involved in a crime or some dishonest activity.

scold [skould] v. 야단치다, 꾸짖다
If you scold someone, you speak angrily to them because they have done something wrong.

slink [sliŋk] v. 살금살금 움직이다
If you slink somewhere, you move there quietly because you do not want to be seen.

peek [pi:k] v. (재빨리) 훔쳐보다; 살짝 보이다; n. 엿보기
If you peek at something or someone, you have a quick look at them, often secretly.

snap [snæp] v. 찰칵 하고 닫히다; 딱 하고 움직이다; (감정 등이) 한 순간에 무너지다; n. 탁 하는 소리
(unsnap v. 그르다, 열다)
To unsnap means to unfasten the snap or catch of something.

holster [hóulstər] n. (벨트에 차는, 가죽) 권총집
A holster is a holder for a small gun, which is worn on a belt around someone's waist or on a strap around their shoulder.

parlor [pá:rlər] n. 상점; 응접실, 거실
Parlor is used in the names of some types of shops which provide a service, rather than selling things.

trunk [trʌŋk] n. (코끼리의) 코; 나무의 몸통; 트렁크 (가방)
An elephant's trunk is its very long nose that it uses to lift food and water to its mouth.

scoop [sku:p] v. (큰 숟가락 등으로) 뜨다; 재빨리 들어올리다; n. 국자; 한 숟가락(의 양)
If you scoop something from a container, you remove it with something such as a spoon.

whip [hwip] v. (크림 등을) 휘젓다; 격렬하게 움직이다; 휙 빼내다; n. 채찍
When you whip something liquid such as cream or an egg, you stir it very fast until it is thick or stiff.

spot [spat] v. 발견하다, 찾다, 알아채다; n. (작은) 점; (특정한) 곳
If you spot something or someone, you notice them.

counter [káuntər] n. (은행·상점 등의) 계산대, 판매대; 반작용, 반대; v. 반박하다
In a place such as a shop or café a counter is a long narrow table or flat surface at which customers are served.

skulk [skʌlk] v. (나쁜 짓을 꾸미며) 몰래 숨다
If you skulk somewhere, you hide or move around quietly because you do not want to be seen.

daylight [déilait] n. 낮, 주간; (낮의) 햇빛, 일광
Daylight is the period of time during the day when it is light.

hit the road idiom 길을 나서다; 출발하다
If you hit the road, you leave a place or begin a journey.

innocent [ínəsənt] a. 순진한; 무죄인, 결백한; 무고한; 악의 없는 (innocently ad. 천진난만하게)
If you say that someone does or says something innocently, you mean that they are pretending not to know something about a situation.

pal [pæl] n. 이봐; 친구
Pal is used when you are talking to a man, sometimes in a friendly way but more often to a man who is annoying you.

notice [nóutis] v. 알아채다, 인지하다; 주의하다; n. 신경씀, 주목, 알아챔
If you notice something or someone, you become aware of them.

toddler [tádlər] n. 걸음마를 배우는 아이, 유아
A toddler is a young child who has only just learned to walk or who still walks unsteadily with small, quick steps.

cling [kliŋ] v. 꼭 붙잡다, 매달리다; 들러붙다; 애착을 갖다
If you cling to someone or something, you hold onto them tightly.

awful [ɔ́:fəl] a. 끔찍한, 지독한; (정도가) 대단한, 아주 심한
If you look or feel awful, you look or feel ill.

jump to conclusions idiom 성급한 결론을 내리다, 속단하다
If you say that someone jumps to a conclusion, you are critical of them because they decide too quickly that something is true, when they do not know all the facts.

mutter [mʌ́tər] v. 중얼거리다; 투덜거리다; n. 중얼거림
If you mutter, you speak very quietly so that you cannot easily be heard, often because you are complaining about something.

buddy [bʌ́di] n. 친구
A buddy is a close friend, usually a male friend of a man.

joint [dʒɔint] n. 가게; 관절; 연결 부위; a. 공동의, 합동의
You can refer to a cheap place where people go for some form of entertainment as a joint.

tousle [tauzl] v. (머리를) 헝클어뜨리다
If you tousle someone's hair, you move your hand backward and forward through it as a way of showing your affection toward them.

fur [fə:r] n. (동물의) 털; 모피
Fur is the thick and usually soft hair that grows on the bodies of many mammals.

goofy [gúːfi] a. 바보 같은, 얼빠진
If you describe someone or something as goofy, you think they are rather silly or ridiculous.

crush [krʌʃ] v. (자신감이나 행복을) 짓밟다; 으스러뜨리다; 밀어 넣다; n. 홀딱 반함; 군중
If you are crushed by something, it upsets you a great deal.

hood [hud] n. (외투 등에 달린) 모자; (자동차 등의) 덮개
A hood is a part of a coat which you can pull up to cover your head.

costume [kástjuːm] n. 의상, 복장; 분장
An actor's or performer's costume is the set of clothes they wear while they are performing.

toot [tuːt] n. 빵, 삑 (하는 경적·호루라기 소리); v. (빵 하고 자동차) 경적을 울리다
A toot is a short, sharp sound made by a horn, trumpet, or similar instrument.

tuck [tʌk] v. 집어 넣다, 끼워 넣다; 밀어넣다; n. 주름, 단
If you tuck something somewhere, you put it there so that it is safe, comfortable, or neat.

sign [sain] n. 표지판, 간판; 징후; 몸짓, 신호; v. 서명하다; 신호를 보내다
A sign is a piece of wood, metal, or plastic with words or pictures on it. Signs give you information about something, or give you a warning or an instruction.

reserve [rizə́ːrv] v. (권한 등을) 갖다; 예약하다; n. 비축(물); 신중함
If you say that you reserve the right to do something, you mean that you will do it if you feel that it is necessary.

beat it idiom 꺼져
If you say 'beat it' to someone, you want them to go away immediately.

hold up idiom (~의 흐름을) 지연시키다; ~을 떠받치다
If you hold up someone or something, you block or delay the progress of them.

annoyed [ənɔ́id] a. 짜증이 난, 악이 오른
If you are annoyed, you are fairly angry about something.

march [maːrtʃ] v. (단호한 태도로 급히) 걸어가다; 행진하다; n. 행군, 행진; 3월
If you say that someone marches somewhere, you mean that they walk there quickly and in a determined way, for example because they are angry.

flash [flæʃ] v. 휙 내보이다; 휙 움직이다; (잠깐) 비치다, 번쩍이다; n. 섬광, 번쩍임; 순간
If you flash something such as an identity card, you show it to people quickly and then put it away again.

customer [kʌ́stəmər] n. 손님, 고객
A customer is someone who buys goods or services, especially from a shop.

snot [snat] n. 콧물
Snot is the substance that is produced inside your nose.

mucus [mjú:kəs] n. 점액
Mucus is a thick liquid that is produced in some parts of your body, for example the inside of your nose.

glove [glʌv] v. 장갑을 끼다; n. 장갑 (ungloved a. 장갑을 끼지 않은)
To unglove means to remove a glove or gloves from a hand.

violate [váiəlèit] v. 위반하다; 침해하다; 훼손하다 (violation n. 위반, 위배)
If someone violates an agreement, law, or promise, they break it.

big deal [bíg dí:l] n. 대단한 것, 큰 일
If you say that something is a big deal, you mean that it is important or significant in some way.

let off idiom (처벌하지 않거나 가벼운 처벌로) ~를 봐주다
If you let someone off, you punish them lightly for something wrong they have done or not punish them at all.

stare [stɛər] v. 빤히 쳐다보다, 응시하다; n. 빤히 쳐다보기, 응시
If you stare at someone or something, you look at them for a long time.

dig [dig] v. (dug–dug) (무엇을 찾기 위해) 뒤지다; 찌르다; (구멍 등을) 파다; n. 쿡 찌르기
If you dig into something such as a deep container, you put your hand in it to search for something.

disbelief [dìsbilí:f] n. 믿기지 않음, 불신감
Disbelief is not believing that something is true or real.

lean [li:n] v. 기울이다, (몸을) 숙이다; ~에 기대다; a. 군살이 없는, 호리호리한
When you lean in a particular direction, you bend your body in that direction.

slap [slæp] v. 털썩 놓다; (손바닥으로) 철썩 때리다; n. 철썩 때리기, 치기
If you slap something onto a surface, you put it there quickly, roughly, or carelessly.

treat [tri:t] n. 대접, 한턱; 즐거움을 주는 것;
v. (특정한 태도로) 대하다; 치료하다, 처치하다; 대접하다, 한턱내다
If you say that something is your treat, you mean that you are paying for it as a treat for someone else.

burn up idiom ~를 분통 터지게 하다
If someone or something burns you up, they make you very angry.

folk [fouk] n. (pl.) (일반적인) 사람들; (pl.) 여러분, 얘들아; a. 민속의, 전통적인; 민중의
You can refer to people as folk or folks.

articulate [a:rtíkjulət] a. (생각·느낌을) 잘 표현하는;
v. (생각·감정을) 분명히 표현하다; 또렷이 말하다
If you describe someone as articulate, you mean that they are able to express their thoughts and ideas easily and well.

fellow [félou] n. 녀석, 친구; 동료; a. 동료의
A fellow is a man or boy.

rare [rɛər] a. 드문, 보기 힘든; 진귀한, 희귀한
An event or situation that is rare does not occur very often.

patronizing [péitrənàiziŋ] a. 잘난 체하는
If someone is patronizing, they speak or behave toward you in a way that seems friendly, but which shows that they think they are superior to you.

sarcasm [sá:rkæzm] n. 빈정댐, 비꼼
Sarcasm is speech or writing which actually means the opposite of what it seems to say. Sarcasm is usually intended to mock or insult someone.

evident [évədənt] a. 분명한, 눈에 띄는
If something is evident, you notice it easily and clearly.

tone [toun] n. 어조, 말투; (글 등의) 분위기; 음색
Someone's tone is a quality in their voice which shows what they are feeling or thinking.

bend [bend] v. (bent–bent) (몸·머리를) 굽히다, 숙이다; 구부리다; n. (도로·강의) 굽이, 굽은 곳
When you bend, you move the top part of your body downward and forward.

paw [pɔ:] n. (동물의) 발; v. 빌로 긁다; (함부로) 건드리다
The paws of an animal such as a cat, dog, or bear are its feet, which have claws for gripping things and soft pads for walking on.

adorable [ədɔ́:rəbl] a. 사랑스러운
If you say that someone or something is adorable, you are emphasizing that they are very attractive and you feel great affection for them.

a spring in one's step idiom 발걸음의 경쾌함
If you walk with or have a spring in your step, you walk energetically in a way that shows you are feeling happy and confident.

CHAPTERS 7 & 8

1. **What had the foxes done with the Jumbo-pop that Judy had bought for them?**

   A. They had thrown it away in the trash.

   B. They had shared it together on a park bench.

   C. They had brought it to a polar bear in Tundratown.

   D. They had melted it down and made pawpsicles to sell.

2. **Why did the foxes visit Little Rodentia after Tundratown?**

   A. They wanted to visit some of their rat friends.

   B. They wanted to sell the used pawpsicle sticks.

   C. They wanted to buy from a mouse ice cream parlor.

   D. They wanted to take a shortcut to another part of town.

3. Which of the following was NOT a reason that Judy wanted to arrest Nick?

    A. False advertising

    B. Selling food without a permit

    C. Stealing from a police officer

    D. Transporting undeclared commerce

4. How did Nick feel about Judy's dreams of coming to Zootopia?

    A. He thought Judy's dreams could come true with hard work.

    B. He wanted to help Judy become a real cop instead of a meter maid.

    C. He didn't really think that everyone could be whatever they wanted to be.

    D. He thought that she already missed her parents and wanted to go back to Bunnyburrow.

5. Why were Judy's parents excited when they saw her over the video chat?

    A. They saw her meter maid uniform.

    B. They noticed that she was smiling.

    C. They liked the look of her new apartment.

    D. They thought her neighbors looked friendly.

Check Your Reading Speed
1분에 몇 단어를 읽는지 리딩 속도를 측정해보세요.

$$\frac{971 \text{ words}}{\text{reading time ( ) sec}} \times 60 = (\quad) \text{ WPM}$$

Build Your Vocabulary

notice [nóutis] v. 알아채다, 인지하다; 주의하다; n. 신경씀, 주목, 알아챔
If you notice something or someone, you become aware of them.

block [blak] n. 구역, 블록; 사각형 덩어리; v. 막다, 차단하다; 방해하다
A block in a town is an area of land with streets on all its sides.

toot [tu:t] n. 빵, 삑 (하는 경적·호루라기 소리); v. (빵 하고 자동차) 경적을 울리다
A toot is a short, sharp sound made by a horn, trumpet, or similar instrument.

wave [weiv] v. (손·팔을) 흔들다; 흔들리다; 손짓하다; n. 파도, 물결; (팔·손·몸을) 흔들기
If you wave or wave your hand, you move your hand from side to side in the air, usually in order to say hello or goodbye to someone.

melt [melt] v. 녹다; (감정 등이) 누그러지다; n. 용해
When a solid substance melts or when you melt it, it changes to a liquid, usually because it has been heated.

channel [ʧænl] v. (물·빛 등을) 보내다; (돈·감정·생각 등을) (~에) 쏟다; n. (텔레비전·라디오의) 채널
If you channel something such as water, you send it along a passage.

jug [dʒʌg] n. 주전자, 병; 항아리
A jug is a cylindrical container with a handle and is used for holding and pouring liquids.

furrow [fɔ́:rou] v. (미간을) 찡그리다; (밭에) 고랑을 만들다; n. 깊은 주름; 고랑
If someone furrows their brow or forehead or if it furrows, deep folds appear in it because the person is annoyed, unhappy, or confused.

brow [brau] n. 이마; (pl.) 눈썹
Your brow is your forehead.

van [væn] n. 승합차; 밴
A van is a small or medium-sized road vehicle with one row of seats at the front and a space for carrying goods behind.

confuse [kənfjúːz] v. (사람을) 혼란시키다; 혼동하다 (confused a. 혼란스러워하는)
If you are confused, you do not know exactly what is happening or what to do.

hop [hap] v. 급히 움직이다; 깡충깡충 뛰다; n. 깡충깡충 뛰기
(hop in idiom 자동차에 뛰어 올라타다)
If you hop somewhere, you move there quickly or suddenly.

section [sékʃən] n. 구역; 부분; (조직의) 부서; v. 구분하다, 구획하다
A section of something is one of the parts into which it is divided or from which it is formed.

mold [mould] n. 주형, 틀; 유형; v. (틀에 넣어) 만들다; (성격·의견 등에) 강한 영향을 주다
A mold is a hollow container that you pour liquid into. When the liquid becomes solid, it takes the same shape as the mold.

pour [pɔːr] v. 붓다, 따르다; 마구 쏟아지다; (대량으로) 쏟아져 들어오다
If you pour a liquid or other substance, you make it flow steadily out of a container by holding the container at an angle.

dozen [dʌzn] n. (pl.) 다수, 여러 개; 12개; 십여 개
If you refer to dozens of things or people, you are emphasizing that there are very many of them.

scandalize [skǽndəlàiz] v. 분개하게 하다; 아연 실색케 하다
If something scandalizes people, they are shocked or offended by it.

set up idiom ~을 세우다; (기계·장비를) 설치하다
If you set up something, you build it or put it somewhere.

stand [stænd] n. 가판대, 좌판; (경기장의) 관중석; v. 서다, 서 있다; (어떤 위치에) 세우다
A stand is a small shop or stall, outdoors or in a large public building.

mark up idiom ~의 가격을 인상하다 (marked-up a. 값을 올린)
To mark something up means to increase the price of it, especially something that you bought for a lower price.

bark [baːrk] v. (명령·질문 등을) 빽 내지르다; (개가) 짖다; n. (개 등이) 짖는 소리; 나무껍질
If you bark at someone, you shout at them aggressively in a loud, rough voice.

treat [triːt] n. 즐거움을 주는 것; 대접, 한턱;
v. (특정한 태도로) 대하다; 치료하다, 처치하다; 대접하다, 한턱내다
If you give someone a treat, you buy or arrange something special for them which they will enjoy.

instant [ínstənt] n. 순간, 아주 짧은 동안; a. 즉각적인 (in an instant idiom 곧, 당장)
An instant is an extremely short period of time.

freeze [friːz] v. 얼다; (두려움 등으로 몸이) 얼어붙다; n. 동결; 한파 (frozen a. 냉동된)
Frozen food has been preserved by being kept at a very low temperature.

dessert [dizə́ːrt] n. 디저트, 후식
Dessert is something sweet, such as fruit or a pudding, that you eat at the end of a meal.

recycle [riːsáikl] v. 재활용하다; 다시 이용하다 (recycling bin n. 재활용품 쓰레기통)
If you recycle things that have already been used, such as bottles or sheets of paper, you process them so that they can be used again.

bin [bin] n. 쓰레기통; (뚜껑 달린) 큰 상자
A bin is a container that you put rubbish in.

adorable [ədɔ́ːrəbl] a. 사랑스러운
If you say that someone or something is adorable, you are emphasizing that they are very attractive and you feel great affection for them.

toddler [tádlər] n. 걸음마를 배우는 아이, 유아
A toddler is a young child who has only just learned to walk or who still walks unsteadily with small, quick steps.

bundle [bʌndl] n. 묶음, 다발; 꾸러미, 보따리; v. ~을 마구 싸 보내다; 무리 지어 가다
If you refer to a bundle of things, you are emphasizing that there is a wide range of them.

plop [plap] v. 털썩 떨어뜨리다; 털썩 주저앉다; n. 퐁당 (하는 소리)
If something plops somewhere, it drops there with a soft, gentle sound.

construction [kənstrʌ́kʃən] n. 건설, 공사; 건축물
Construction is the building of things such as houses, factories, roads, and bridges.

lumber [lʌ́mbər] n. 목재, 재목; v. (육중한 덩치로) 느릿느릿 움직이다
Lumber consists of trees and large pieces of wood that have been roughly cut up.

shrug off idiom ~을 대수롭지 않게 취급하다
If you shrug something off, you treat it as if it is not important or not a problem.

haul [hɔ:l] v. 운반하다; 끌다; (몸을) 간신히 움직이다; n. 세게 잡아당김
If you haul something which is heavy or difficult to move, you move it using a lot of effort.

awe [ɔ:] n. 경외감, 외경심; v. 경외심을 갖게 하다
Awe is the feeling of respect and amazement that you have when you are faced with something wonderful and often rather frightening.

diaper [dáiəpər] n. 기저귀
A diaper is a piece of soft towel or paper, which you fasten round a baby's bottom in order to soak up its urine and faeces.

jokingly [dʒóukiŋli] ad. 농담 삼아, 장난으로
If you say or do something jokingly, you say or do it with the intention of amusing someone, rather than with any serious meaning or intention.

bite [bait] v. (이빨로) 물다; 베어 물다; n. 물기; 한 입; 소량
If an animal or person bites you, they use their teeth to hurt or injure you.

ciao [ʧau] int. 안녕, 잘 가
Some people say 'Ciao' as an informal way of saying goodbye to someone who they expect to see again soon.

blare [blɛər] v. (소리를) 요란하게 울리다; n. 요란한 소리
If something such as a siren or radio blares or if you blare it, it makes a loud, unpleasant noise.

stand up for idiom ~을 옹호하다, ~을 지지하다
If you stand up for someone or something, you defend or support a particular idea or a person who is being criticized or attacked.

yell [jel] v. 고함치다, 소리 지르다; n. 고함, 외침
If you yell, you shout loudly, usually because you are excited, angry, or in pain.

hustle [hʌsl] n. 사기; 법석, 혼잡; v. (사람을 거칠게) 떠밀다; (불법적으로) 팔다
A hustle is a dishonest way of making money.

sweetheart [swíːthàːrt] n. (애정을 담아 부르는 호칭으로) 자기, 애야
You call someone sweetheart if you are very fond of them.

whip [hwip] v. 격렬하게 움직이다; (크림 등을) 휘젓다; 휙 빼내다; n. 채찍
(whip around idiom 갑자기 방향을 바꾸다)
If you whip around, you move fast or suddenly in a specified direction.

tail [teil] n. (동물의) 꼬리; 끝부분; v. 미행하다
The tail of an animal, bird, or fish is the part extending beyond the end of its body.

catch up idiom 따라잡다, 따라가다
If you catch up with someone or something, you reach them ahead of you by going faster than them.

stroll [stroul] v. 거닐다, 산책하다; n. (한가로이) 거닐기, 산책
If you stroll somewhere, you walk there in a slow, relaxed way.

slick [slik] a. 교활한; (겉만) 번드르르한
A slick person speaks easily in a way that is likely to convince people, but is not sincere.

arrest [ərést] n. 체포; 저지, 정지; v. 체포하다; 막다 (be under arrest idiom 체포되다)
An arrest is the action of seizing someone to take into legal custody, as by officers of the law.

gee [dʒiː] int. (놀람·감탄을 나타내어) 이런, 어머나, 아이 깜짝이야
People sometimes say 'gee' to emphasize a reaction or remark.

permit [pərmít] n. 허가증; v. 허락하다, 허용하다
A permit is an official document which says that you may do something.

transport [trænspɔ́ːrt] v. 수송하다; 실어 나르다; n. 수송; 운송 수단
To transport people or goods somewhere is to take them from one place to another in a vehicle.

declare [diklέər] v. (소득·과세 물품 등을) 신고하다; 선언하다, 공표하다; 분명히 말하다
(undeclared a. (과세) 신고되지 않은)
Undeclared goods are goods that you bring illegally into a country without telling the customs authorities.

commerce [káməːrs] n. 무역; 상업
Commerce is the activities and procedures involved in buying and selling things.

borough [bɔ́ːrou] n. 자치구
A borough is a town, or a district within a large town, which has its own council.

advertise [ǽdvərtàiz] v. 광고하다, 알리다
If you advertise something such as a product, an event, or a job, you tell people about it in newspapers, on television, or on posters in order to encourage them to buy the product, go to the event, or apply for the job.

receipt [risíːt] n. 영수증; 수령, 인수
A receipt is a piece of paper that you get from someone as proof that they have received money or goods from you.

smug [smʌg] a. 의기양양한, 우쭐해 하는 (smugly ad. 잘난 체하며)
If you say that someone is smug, you are criticizing the fact they seem very pleased with how good, clever, or lucky they are.

refrain [rifréin] v. 삼가다, 자제하다
If you refrain from doing something, you deliberately do not do it.

assume [əsúːm] v. (사실일 것으로) 추정하다; (특질·양상을) 띠다
If you assume that something is true, you imagine that it is true, sometimes wrongly.

choke [ʧouk] v. 채우다, 막다; 숨이 막히다; (목소리가) 잠기다; n. 숨이 막힘, 질식
If a place is choked with things or people, it is full of them and they prevent movement in it.

county [káunti] n. 자치주
A county is a region of Britain, Ireland, or the USA which has its own local government.

tone [toun] n. 어조, 말투; (글 등의) 분위기; 음색
Someone's tone is a quality in their voice which shows what they are feeling or thinking.

bold [bould] a. 뻔뻔스러운; 용감한, 대담한; 선명한, 굵은 (boldly ad. 뻔뻔스럽게)
Someone who is bold is not shy or embarrassed in the company of other people.

naïve [naːíːv] a. 순진한; 천진난만한
If you describe someone as naïve, you think they lack experience and so expect things to be easy or people to be honest or kind.

hick [hik] n. 시골뜨기, 촌놈
If you refer to someone as a hick, you are saying in a rude way that you think they are uneducated and stupid because they come from the countryside.

predator [prédətər] n. 포식자, 포식 동물; 약탈자
A predator is an animal that kills and eats other animals.

prey [prei] n. 먹이, 사냥감; 희생자, 피해자
A creature's prey are the creatures that it hunts and eats in order to live.

harmony [hɑ́:rməni] n. 조화, 화합; 화음
If people are living in harmony with each other, they are living together peacefully rather than fighting or arguing.

get along idiom 사이좋게 지내다; 어울리다
If people get along, they like each other and are friendly to each other.

cop [kap] n. 경찰관
A cop is a policeman or policewoman.

emotional [imóuʃənl] a. 감정적인; 정서의, 감정의
An emotional situation or issue is one that causes people to have strong feelings.

literal [lítərəl] a. 문자 그대로의; (번역이) 직역의
If you describe something as the literal truth or a literal fact, you are emphasizing that it is true.

squalor [skwálər] n. 불결한 상태
You can refer to very dirty, unpleasant conditions as squalor.

tail between one's legs idiom 창피해 하며, 기가 죽어서
If you say that you have your tail between your legs, you are emphasizing that you feel defeated and ashamed.

speechless [spíːʧlis] a. 말을 못 하는
If you are speechless, you are temporarily unable to speak, usually because something has shocked you.

knock [nak] v. 치다, 부딪치다; (문 등을) 두드리다; n. 문 두드리는 소리; 부딪침
If you knock something, you touch or hit it roughly, especially so that it falls or moves.

crush [krʌʃ] v. (자신감이나 행복을) 짓밟다; 으스러뜨리다; 밀어 넣다; n. 홀딱 반함; 군중
If you are crushed by something, it upsets you a great deal.

pull together idiom 정신 차리다; 가라앉다; 함께 일하다, 협력하다
If you pull it together or pull yourself together, you gain control of your feelings and start to act in a calm and sensible way.

jerk [dʒə:rk] n. 얼간이; 홱 움직임; v. 홱 움직이다
If you call someone a jerk, you are insulting them because you think they are stupid or you do not like them.

gut [ɡʌt] n. (pl.) 배짱; 배; 소화관; v. 내부를 파괴하다; a. 직감에 따른
Guts is the will and courage to do something which is difficult or unpleasant, or which might have unpleasant results.

hustler [hʌ́slər] n. 사기꾼
If you refer to someone as a hustler, you mean that they try to earn money or gain an advantage from situations they are in by using dishonest or illegal methods.

sly [slai] a. 교활한, 음흉한; 다 알고 있다는 듯한
If you describe someone as sly, you disapprove of them because they keep their feelings or intentions hidden and are clever at deceiving people.

dumb [dʌm] a. 멍청한, 바보 같은; 말을 못 하는
If you call a person dumb, you mean that they are stupid or foolish.

ankle [ǽŋkl] n. 발목 (ankle-deep idiom 깊이가 발목까지 오는)
Your ankle is the joint where your foot joins your leg.

gooey [gu:i] a. 끈적끈적한, 들러붙는
If you describe a food or other substance as gooey, you mean that it is very soft and sticky.

sigh [sai] v. 한숨을 쉬다, 한숨짓다; 탄식하듯 말하다; n. 한숨
When you sigh, you let out a deep breath, as a way of expressing feelings such as disappointment, tiredness, or pleasure.

dismay [disméi] n. 실망, 경악; v. 경악하게 하다, 크게 실망시키다
Dismay is a strong feeling of fear, worry, or sadness that is caused by something unpleasant and unexpected.

obnoxious [əbnákʃəs] a. 아주 불쾌한, 몹시 기분 나쁜 (obnoxiously ad. 불쾌하게)
If you describe someone or something as obnoxious, you think that they are very unpleasant.

supervisor [súːpərvàizər] n. 감독관, 관리자
A supervisor is a person who supervises activities or people, especially workers or students.

hang in there idiom 버티다, 견뎌내다
If you tell someone to hang in there or to hang on in there, you are encouraging them to keep trying to do something and not to give up even though it might be difficult.

frustrate [frʌ́streit] v. 좌절감을 주다, 불만스럽게 하다; 방해하다

(frustrated a. 좌절감을 느끼는, 불만스러워 하는)

If something frustrates you, it upsets or angers you because you are unable to do anything about the problems it creates.

set about idiom ~을 시작하다

If you set about doing something such as a task or an activity, you begin it, especially with energy or enthusiasm.

Check Your Reading Speed

1분에 몇 단어를 읽는지 리딩 속도를 측정해보세요.

$$\frac{450 \text{ words}}{\text{reading time ( ) sec}} \times 60 = (\quad) \text{ WPM}$$

Build Your Vocabulary

drag [dræg] v. 끌다, 끌고 가다; 힘들게 움직이다; n. 끌기, 당기기; 장애물
If you drag something, you pull it along the ground, often with difficulty.

switch [switʃ] v. 전환하다, 바꾸다; n. 스위치; 전환
If you switch to something different, for example to a different system, task, or subject of conversation, you change to it from what you were doing or saying before.

station [stéiʃən] n. 방송 (프로); 역; 정거장; (관청·시설 등의) 서(署); v. 배치하다
If you talk about a particular radio or television station, you are referring to the programs broadcast by a particular radio or television company.

depressing [diprésiŋ] a. 우울하게 하는, 우울한
Something that is depressing makes you feel sad and disappointed.

pop [pap] v. 급히 놓다; 펑 하는 소리가 나다; 잡다; n. 팝(뮤직); 펑 (하고 터지는 소리)
If you pop something somewhere, you put it there quickly.

microwave [máikrouwèiv] n. (= microwave oven) 전자레인지; v. 전자레인지에 요리하다
A microwave or a microwave oven is an oven which cooks food very quickly by electromagnetic radiation rather than by heat.

beep [bi:p] n. 삑 (하는 소리); v. 삐 소리를 내다; (경적을) 울리다
A beep is a short, loud sound like that made by a car horn or a telephone answering machine.

peel [pi:l] v. (층·덮개 등을) 벗기다; 껍질을 벗기다; n. (과일·채소의) 껍질
If you peel off something that has been sticking to a surface or if it peels off, it comes away from the surface.

reveal [riví:l] v. (보이지 않던 것을) 드러내 보이다; (비밀 등을) 밝히다
If you reveal something that has been out of sight, you uncover it so that people can see it.

shrivel [ʃrívəl] v. 쪼글쪼글해지다; 쪼글쪼글하게 만들다
When something shrivels or when something shrivels it, it becomes dryer and smaller, often with lines in its surface, as a result of losing the water it contains.

droop [dru:p] v. 아래로 처지다; 풀이 죽다; (기가) 꺾이다
If something droops, it hangs or leans downward with no strength or firmness.

chat [ʧæt] n. 이야기, 대화; v. 이야기를 나누다, 수다를 떨다 (video chat n. 화상 채팅)
A video chat is a face-to-face conversation held over the Internet by means of webcams and dedicated software.

sigh [sai] v. 한숨을 쉬다, 한숨짓다; 탄식하듯 말하다; n. 한숨
When you sigh, you let out a deep breath, as a way of expressing feelings such as disappointment, tiredness, or pleasure.

force [fɔ:rs] v. 억지로 ~하다; ~를 강요하다; n. 원동력; 영향력; 힘
If you force a smile or a laugh, you manage to smile or laugh, but with an effort because you are unhappy.

upbeat [ʌ́pbì:t] a. 긍정적인, 낙관적인
If people or their opinions are upbeat, they are cheerful and hopeful about a situation.

sweetheart [swí:thà:rt] n. (애정을 담아 부르는 호칭으로) 자기, 얘야
You call someone sweetheart if you are very fond of them.

peer [piər] v. 유심히 보다, 눈여겨보다; n. 또래
If you peer at something, you look at it very hard, usually because it is difficult to see clearly.

backpedal [bǽkpèdl] v. 말을 바꾸다; 약속대로 안 하다; 후퇴하다
If you backpedal, you express a different or less forceful opinion about something from the one you have previously expressed.

temporary [témpərèri] a. 일시적인, 임시의
Something that is temporary lasts for only a limited time.

exclaim [ikskléim] v. 소리치다, 외치다
If you exclaim, you cry out suddenly in surprise, strong emotion, or pain.

prayer [prɛər] n. 기도; 기도문; 간절히 원하는 것
You can refer to a strong hope that you have as your prayer.

overjoyed [òuvərdʒɔ́id] a. 매우 기뻐하는
If you are overjoyed, you are extremely pleased about something.

glorious [glɔ́:riəs] a. 대단히 즐거운; 영광스러운; 눈부시게 아름다운
If you describe something as glorious, you are emphasizing that it is wonderful and it makes you feel very happy.

chant [ʧænt] v. 구호를 외치다, 연호하다; n. (연이어 외치는) 구호
If you chant something or if you chant, you repeat the same words over and over again.

hang up idiom 전화를 끊다
If you hang up the phone or hang up on someone, you end a telephone conversation, often very suddenly.

bicker [bíkər] v. (사소한 일로) 다투다
When people bicker, they argue or quarrel about unimportant things.

exhaust [igzɔ́:st] v. 기진맥진하게 하다; 다 써 버리다; n. (자동차 등의) 배기가스
(exhausted a. 기진맥진한)
If something exhausts you, it makes you so tired, either physically or mentally, that you have no energy left.

settle [setl] v. 자리 잡다, 정착하다; 놓다; 해결하다; 진정시키다
(settle in for the night idiom 차분히 하룻밤을 묵다)
If you settle in, you make yourself comfortable in a place because you are going to stay there for a long time.

CHAPTERS 9 & 10

1. **Which of the following was NOT something that happened when the weasel thief went into Little Rodentia?**
   A. Judy struggled to protect each building that the weasel knocked.
   B. Judy pushed the weasel off the train but lost him.
   C. Judy was small enough to fit through the gate to the tiny community.
   D. Judy caught a donut sign that the weasel had thrown and stopped it from hitting some rodents.

2. **How did Judy capture the weasel thief?**
   A. She pushed him in front of the train.
   B. She trapped him in a tiny mouse house.
   C. She used the huge donut sign to capture him.
   D. She forced the weasel out of Little Rodentia into other cops.

3. What chance did Chief Bogo give Judy?

   A. He gave her a chance of being promoted.

   B. He gave her two days to find Emmitt Otterton.

   C. He gave her a chance to do parking duty in a different neighborhood.

   D. He gave her two days of working at the front desk with Clawhauser.

4. How did Judy find her first lead on the case of the missing otter?

   A. She noticed a pawpsicle in the picture.

   B. She noticed a baby stroller in the picture.

   C. She noticed Nick and Finnick in the picture.

   D. She noticed Nick and his son in the picture.

5. What did Judy use to threaten to arrest Nick?

   A. Murder

   B. Felony tax evasion

   C. Endangerment of a child

   D. Impersonation of a police officer

Check Your Reading Speed

1분에 몇 단어를 읽는지 리딩 속도를 측정해보세요.

$$\frac{1{,}650 \text{ words}}{\text{reading time } (\quad) \text{ sec}} \times 60 = (\quad\quad) \text{ WPM}$$

Build Your Vocabulary

expire [ikspáiər] v. (기한이) 만료되다, 만기가 되다
When something such as a contract, deadline, or visa expires, it comes to an end or is no longer valid.

plunk [plʌŋk] v. 탁 하고 내려놓다; 털썩 앉다; n. 쿵 (하는 소리)
If you plunk something somewhere, you put it or drop it there heavily and carelessly.

ding [diŋ] v. 딩동 하는 소리를 내다; (차체 등을) 쿵 들이받다; n. 딩동, 땡 (하는 소리)
If something dings, it makes a ringing sound.

scribble [skribl] v. 갈겨쓰다, 휘갈기다; 낙서하다; n. 낙서
If you scribble something, you write it quickly and roughly.

tiny [táini] a. 아주 작은
Something or someone that is tiny is extremely small.

windshield [wíndʃiːld] n. (자동차 등의) 앞 유리
The windshield of a car or other vehicle is the glass window at the front through which the driver looks.

tax [tæks] n. 세금; v. 세금을 부과하다, 과세하다
Tax is an amount of money that you have to pay to the government so that it can pay for public services.

salary [sǽləri] n. 급여, 월급
A salary is the money that someone is paid each month by their employer, especially when they are in a profession such as teaching, law, or medicine.

bang [bæŋ] v. 쾅 하고 치다; 쾅 하고 닫다; 쿵 하고 찧다; n. 쾅 (하는 소리)
If you bang on something or if you bang it, you hit it hard, making a loud noise.

steer [stiər] v. (보트·자동차 등을) 조종하다; (특정 방향으로) 움직이다
When you steer a car, boat, or plane, you control it so that it goes in the direction that you want.

wheel [hwiːl] n. (자동차 등의) 핸들; 바퀴; v. (바퀴 달린 것을) 밀다; 태우고 가다
(steering wheel n. (자동차의) 핸들)
In a car or other vehicle, the steering wheel is the wheel which the driver holds when he or she is driving.

honk [haŋk] v. (자동차 경적을) 울리다; (기러기가) 울다; n. 빵빵 (자동차 경적 소리)
If you honk the horn of a vehicle or if the horn honks, you make the horn produce a short loud sound.

mutter [mʌ́tər] v. 중얼거리다; 투덜거리다; n. 중얼거림
If you mutter, you speak very quietly so that you cannot easily be heard, often because you are complaining about something.

frantic [frǽntik] a. (두려움·걱정으로) 제정신이 아닌; 정신없이 서두는
If you are frantic, you are behaving in a wild and uncontrolled way because you are frightened or worried.

pound [paund] v. (여러 차례) 치다, 두드리다; 쿵쾅거리며 걷다
If you pound something or pound on it, you hit it with great force, usually loudly and repeatedly.

grievance [gríːvəns] n. 불만, 고충
If you have a grievance about something that has happened or been done, you believe that it was unfair.

contest [kəntést] ① v. 이의를 제기하다; 경쟁을 벌이다 ② n. 대회, 시합
If you contest a statement or decision, you object to it formally because you think it is wrong or unreasonable.

citation [saitéiʃən] n. (법원) 소환장; 인용구; 인용
A citation is an official order to appear in court.

mechanical [məkǽnikəl] a. (행동이) 기계적인; 기계로 작동되는
(mechanically ad. 기계적으로)
If you describe someone's action as mechanical, you mean that they do it automatically, without thinking about it.

rob [rab] v. (사람·장소를) 도둑질하다
If someone is robbed, they have money or property stolen from them.

get away idiom 도망치다; ~로부터 벗어나다; 휴가를 가다
If you get away from someone or somewhere, you escape from them or there.

snap out of idiom (기분·습관에서) 재빨리 벗어나다; 기운을 차리다, 회복하다
If you snap out of something, you force yourself to stop feeling sad and upset.

chase [ʧeis] v. 뒤쫓다, 추적하다; 추구하다; n. 추적, 추격; 추구함
If you chase someone, or chase after them, you run after them or follow them quickly in order to catch or reach them.

screech [skri:ʧ] v. 끼익 하는 소리를 내다; n. 끼익, 꽥 (하는 날카로운 소리)
If a vehicle screeches somewhere or if its tires screech, its tires make an unpleasant high-pitched noise on the road.

patrol [pətróul] n. 순찰; 순찰대; v. 순찰을 돌다; (특히 위협적으로) 돌아다니다
(patrol car n. 순찰차)
A patrol car is a police car used for patrolling streets and roads.

officer [ɔ́:fisər] n. 순경; 경찰관; 장교
Members of the police force can be referred to as officers.

slide [slaid] v. (slid–slid/slidden) 미끄러지듯이 움직이다; 미끄러지다; 슬며시 넣다; n. 떨어짐; 미끄러짐
If you slide somewhere, you move there smoothly and quietly.

hood [hud] n. (자동차 등의) 덮개; (외투 등에 달린) 모자
The hood of a car is the metal cover over the engine at the front.

rip [rip] v. (재빨리·거칠게) 떼어 내다, 뜯어 내다; (갑자기) 찢다; n. (길게) 찢어진 곳
If you rip something away, you remove it quickly and forcefully.

dibs [dibz] n. 우선권, 자기 차례; (소액의) 돈
If you have dibs on something, you have a right to have or get it from someone, or to use it.

pursuit [pərsú:t] n. 뒤쫓음, 추적; 추구
Someone who is in pursuit of a person, vehicle, or animal is chasing them.

dodge [dadʒ] v. (몸을) 재빨리 움직이다; 기피하다; n. 몸을 홱 피함
If you dodge, you move suddenly, often to avoid being hit, caught, or seen.

duck [dʌk] v. 급히 움직이다; (머리나 몸을) 휙 수그리다; 피하다; n. [동물] 오리
If you duck, you move quickly to a place, especially in order not to be seen.

forceful [fɔ́ːrsfəl] a. 단호한; 강력한; 강압적인 (forcefully ad. 강력하게; 강압적으로)
If you describe someone as forceful, you approve of them because they express their opinions and wishes in a strong, emphatic, and confident way.

rodent [roudnt] n. 설치류
Rodents are small mammals which have sharp front teeth. Rats, mice, and squirrels are rodents.

swerve [swəːrv] v. (갑자기) 방향을 바꾸다
If a vehicle or other moving thing swerves or if you swerve it, it suddenly changes direction, often in order to avoid hitting something.

midair [midέər] n. 공중, 상공
If something happens in midair, it happens in the air, rather than on the ground.

prevent [privént] v. 막다, 예방하다, 방지하다
To prevent something means to ensure that it does not happen.

disaster [dizǽstər] n. 참사, 재난; 엄청난 불행, 재앙
A disaster is a very bad accident such as an earthquake or a plane crash, especially one in which a lot of people are killed.

tip [tip] v. 살짝 건드리다; 기울어지다, 젖혀지다; n. (뾰족한) 끝
If you tip an object or part of your body or if it tips, it moves into a sloping position with one end or side higher than the other.

struggle [strʌgl] v. 애쓰다; 허우적거리다; (~와) 싸우다; n. 투쟁; 싸움, 몸부림
If you struggle to do something, you try hard to do it, even though other people or things may be making it difficult for you to succeed.

leap [liːp] v. (leaped/leapt–leaped/leapt) 뛰다, 뛰어오르다; (서둘러) ~하다; n. 높이뛰기, 도약; 급증
If you leap, you jump high in the air or jump a long distance.

chuckle [ʧʌkl] n. 킬킬거림; 속으로 웃기; v. 킬킬 웃다; 빙그레 웃다
A chuckle is a quiet or suppressed laugh.

give up idiom 포기하다; 그만두다; 단념하다
If you give up, you stop trying to do something, usually because it is too difficult.

barrel [bǽrəl] v. 쏜살같이 달리다; n. (대형) 통
If a vehicle or person is barreling in a particular direction, they are moving very quickly in that direction.

midst [midst] n. 한복판, 중앙, 한가운데
If someone or something is in the midst of a group of people or things, they are among them or surrounded by them.

yank [jæŋk] v. 홱 잡아당기다; n. 홱 잡아당기기
If you yank someone or something somewhere, you pull them there suddenly and with a lot of force.

sign [sain] n. 표지판, 간판; 징후; 몸짓, 신호; v. 서명하다; 신호를 보내다
A sign is a piece of wood, metal, or plastic with words or pictures on it. Signs give you information about something, or give you a warning or an instruction.

fling [fliŋ] v. (flung-flung) (거칠게) 내던지다; (머리·팔 등을) 휘두르다; n. (한바탕) 실컷 즐기기
If you fling something somewhere, you throw it there using a lot of force.

bounce [bauns] v. (공 등이) 튀다, 뛰어오르다; 깡충깡충 뛰다; n. (공 등이) 튐, 튀어 오름; 탄력
When an object such as a ball bounces or when you bounce it, it moves upward from a surface or away from it immediately after hitting it.

fashionable [fǽʃənəbl] a. 유행하는, 유행을 따른; 상류 사회의
Something or someone that is fashionable is popular or approved of at a particular time.

terror [térər] n. 두려움, 공포; 공포의 대상
Terror is very great fear.

crush [krʌʃ] v. 으스러뜨리다; (자신감이나 행복을) 짓밟다; 밀어 넣다; n. 홀딱 반함; 군중
To crush something means to press it very hard so that its shape is destroyed or so that it breaks into pieces.

grateful [gréitfəl] a. 고마워하는, 감사하는 (**gratefully** ad. 감사하여, 기뻐서)
If you are grateful for something that someone has given you or done for you, you have warm, friendly feelings toward them and wish to thank them.

out of the corner of one's eye idiom 곁눈질로; 흘깃 보고
If you see something out of the corner of your eye, you see it but not clearly because it happens to the side of you.

trap [træp] v. (위험한 장소·궁지에) 가두다; (함정으로) 몰아넣다; n. 덫, 올가미; 함정
If you are trapped somewhere, something falls onto you or blocks your way and prevents you from moving or escaping.

pop [pap] v. 잡다; 급히 놓다; 펑 하는 소리가 나다; n. 팝(뮤직); 펑 (하고 터지는 소리)
If the police pop you, they take you into legal custody.

chief [ʧiːf] n. (단체의) 최고위자; 추장, 족장; a. 주된; (계급·직급상) 최고위자인
The chief of an organization is the person who is in charge of it.

principal [prínsəpəl] n. 교장; a. 주요한, 주된
The principal of a school or college is the person in charge of the school or college.

abandon [əbǽndən] v. 버리고 떠나다; 버리다; 그만두다
If you abandon a place, thing, or person, you leave the place, thing, or person permanently or for a long time, especially when you should not do so.

post [poust] n. (근무) 구역; 기둥, 말뚝; 직책; v. (근무 위치에) 배치하다; (안내문 등을) 게시하다
You can use post to refer to the place where a soldier, guard, or other person has been told to remain and to do his or her job.

incite [insáit] v. 선동하다, 조장하다
If someone incites people to behave in a violent or illegal way, they encourage people to behave in that way, usually by making them excited or angry.

scurry [skə́ːri] n. 허둥댐; v. 허둥지둥 가다, 종종걸음을 치다
A scurry is a situation of hurried and confused movement.

reckless [réklis] a. 무모한, 신중하지 못한; 난폭한
If you say that someone is reckless, you mean that they act in a way which shows that they do not care about danger or the effect their behavior will have on other people.

endanger [indéindʒər] v. 위험에 빠뜨리다, 위태롭게 하다 (endangerment n. 위험에 빠뜨리기)
To endanger something or someone means to put them in a situation where they might be harmed or destroyed completely.

criminal [krímənl] n. 범인, 범죄자; a. 범죄의; 형사상의
A criminal is a person who regularly commits crimes.

moldy [móuldi] a. 곰팡이가 핀; 케케묵은
Something that is moldy is covered with mold.

confiscate [kánfəskèit] v. 몰수하다, 압수하다
If you confiscate something from someone, you take it away from them, usually as a punishment.

crook [kruk] n. 사기꾼; v. (손가락이나 팔을) 구부리다
A crook is a dishonest person or a criminal.

varietal [vəráiətl] a. 변종의
Varietal means relating to, characteristic of, designating, or forming a variety, especially a biological variety.

botanical [bətǽnikəl] a. 식물(학)의; n. 식물성 약품
Botanical means involving or relating to plants or the study of plants.

husbandry [hʌ́zbəndri] n. 농업, 농사
Husbandry is farming animals, especially when it is done carefully and well.

intercom [íntərkam] n. 내부 통화 장치, 인터콤
An intercom is a small box with a microphone which is connected to a loudspeaker in another room.

click [klik] v. 딸깍 하는 소리를 내다; (마우스를) 클릭하다; n. 찰칵 (하는 소리); (마우스를) 클릭함
If something clicks or if you click it, it makes a short, sharp sound.

mayor [méiər] n. (시·군 등의) 시장
The mayor of a town or city is the person who has been elected to represent it for a fixed period of time or, in some places, to run its government.

assign [əsáin] v. (사람을) 배치하다; (일·책임 등을) 맡기다; ~의 탓으로 하다
If someone is assigned to a particular place, group, or person, they are sent there, usually in order to work at that place or for that person.

interrupt [ìntərʌ́pt] v. (말·행동을) 방해하다; 중단시키다; 차단하다
If you interrupt someone who is speaking, you say or do something that causes them to stop.

insipid [insípid] a. 재미없는; 맛이 없는
If you describe someone or something as insipid, you mean they are dull and boring.

let go idiom (생각·태도 등을) 버리다, 포기하다; (잡고 있던 것을) 놓다; ~를 풀어주다
To let go means to stop thinking about or being angry about the past or something that happened in the past.

barge [baːrdʒ] v. 밀치고 가다; n. 바지선
If you barge into a place or barge through it, you rush or push into it in a rough and rude way.

trail [treil] v. 뒤를 따라가다; 끌다; 뒤쫓다; n. 자국, 흔적; 자취
If someone trails somewhere, they move there slowly, without any energy or enthusiasm, often following someone else.

wheeze [hwiːz] v. (숨쉬기가 힘이 들어서) 쌕쌕거리다; n. 쌕쌕거리는 소리
If someone wheezes, they breathe with difficulty and make a whistling sound.

plead [pliːd] v. 애원하다; 옹호하다, 주장하다
If you plead with someone to do something, you ask them in an intense, emotional way to do it.

slippery [slípəri] a. 미끄러운, 미끈거리는; 약삭빠른
Something that is slippery is smooth, wet, or oily and is therefore difficult to walk on or to hold.

pant [pænt] v. (숨을) 헐떡이다; n. 헐떡거림
If you pant, you breathe quickly and loudly with your mouth open, because you have been doing something energetic.

florist [flɔ́ːrist] n. 꽃집 주인; 화초 재배자
A florist is a shopkeeper who arranges and sells flowers and sells house plants.

detective [ditéktiv] n. 형사, 수사관; 탐정
A detective is a person, especially a police officer, whose occupation is to investigate and solve crimes.

concern [kənsə́ːrn] n. 우려, 걱정; 관심사; v. 걱정스럽게 하다; 관련되다
Concern is worry about a situation.

disappearance [dìsəpíːərəns] n. 실종; 사라짐, 소실
If you refer to someone's disappearance, you are referring to the fact that nobody knows where they have gone.

explode [iksplóud] v. (갑자기 강한 감정을) 터뜨리다; 터지다, 폭발하다
If someone explodes, they express strong feelings suddenly and violently.

bless you idiom 고맙기도 해라; 세상에, 맙소사
Bless is used in expressions such as 'God bless' or 'bless you' to express affection, thanks, or good wishes.

relieve [rilíːv] v. 안도하게 하다; (불쾌감·고통 등을) 없애 주다; 완화하다 (relieved a. 안도하는)
If you are relieved, you feel happy because something unpleasant has not happened or is no longer happening.

grunt [grʌnt] v. 끙 앓는 소리를 내다; (돼지가) 꿀꿀거리다; n. (사람이) 끙 하는 소리
If you grunt, you make a low sound, especially because you are annoyed or not interested in something.

usher [ʌ́ʃər] v. 안내하다; n. 안내인, 수위
If you usher someone somewhere, you show them where they should go, often by going with them.

furious [fjúəriəs] a. 몹시 화가 난; 맹렬한
Someone who is furious is extremely angry.

fire [faiər] v. 해고하다; 사격하다, 발사하다; (엔진이) 점화되다; n. 화재, 불
If an employer fires you, they dismiss you from your job.

insubordination [ìnsəbɔ̀ːrdənéiʃən] n. 불복종, 반항
Insubordination is a refusal to obey someone of higher rank.

delusion [dilúːʒən] n. 망상; 착각, 오해 (delusions of grandeur n. 과대망상)
If someone has delusions of grandeur, they think and behave as if they are much more important or powerful than they really are.

grandeur [grǽndʒər] n. 장엄함, 위엄
Someone's grandeur is the great importance and social status that they have, or think they have.

assistant [əsístənt] a. 부(副)-, 조(助)-, 보조의; n. 조수, 보조원
Assistant is used in front of titles or jobs to indicate a slightly lower rank.

mammal [mǽməl] n. 포유동물
Mammals are animals such as humans, dogs, lions, and whales. In general, female mammals give birth to babies rather than laying eggs, and feed their young with milk.

include [inklúːd] v. 포함하다; ~을 (~에) 포함시키다 (inclusion n. 포함, 포괄)
Inclusion is the act of making a person or thing part of a group or collection.

initiative [iníʃiətiv] n. 계획; 진취성; 결단력
An initiative is an important act or statement that is intended to solve a problem.

pay off idiom 성공하다, 성과를 올리다; (돈으로) ~를 매수하다
If something that involves risk pays off, it is successful and brings the results that you want.

jazzed [dʒæzd] a. 활기찬, 재미있는, 신나는
If you are jazzed, you are excited.

stick together idiom 함께 뭉치다; 옆에 바싹 붙다
If two or more people stick together, they remain friendly and loyal to one another.

force [fɔːrs] v. 억지로 ~하다; ~를 강요하다; n. 원동력; 영향력; 힘
If you force a smile or a laugh, you manage to smile or laugh, but with an effort because you are unhappy.

strike out idiom 실패하다, 성공하지 못하다
If you strike out, you are unsuccessful in trying to do something.

resign [rizáin] v. 사직하다, 물러나다
If you resign from a job or position, you formally announce that you are leaving it.

nod [nad] v. (고개를) 끄덕이다, 까딱하다; n. (고개를) 끄덕임
If you nod, you move your head downward and upward to show that you are answering 'yes' to a question, or to show agreement, understanding, or approval.

splendid [spléndid] a. 정말 좋은, 훌륭한; 아주 인상적인
If you say that something is splendid, you mean that it is very good.

rush [rʌʃ] v. 급(속)히 움직이다; 서두르다; 재촉하다; n. 혼잡, 분주함
If you rush somewhere, you go there quickly.

retrieve [ritríːv] v. 되찾아오다, 회수하다; 수습하다
If you retrieve something, you get it back from the place where you left it.

folder [fóuldər] n. 서류철, 폴더
A folder is a thin piece of cardboard in which you can keep loose papers.

jaw [dʒɔː] n. 턱
Your jaw is the lower part of your face below your mouth.

disbelief [disbilíːf] n. 믿기지 않음, 불신감
Disbelief is not believing that something is true or real.

lead [liːd] ① n. 실마리, 단서; 선두, 우세; v. 안내하다, 이끌다; 이어지다 ② n. [광물] 납
A lead is a piece of information or an idea which may help people to discover the facts in a situation where many facts are not known.

witness [wítnis] n. 목격자; 증인; v. (사건·사고를) 목격하다; 증명하다
A witness to an event such as an accident or crime is a person who saw it.

resource [ríːsɔːrs] n. 수단; 재료; 자원, 재원; v. 자원을 제공하다
The resources of an organization or person are the materials, money, and other things that they have and can use in order to function properly.

stake [steik] v. (돈 등을) 걸다; 말뚝을 받치다; n. 말뚝; 지분; (내기 등에) 건 것
If you stake something such as your money or your reputation on the result of something, you risk your money or reputation on it.

crack [kræk] v. (문제나 난국을) 해결하다; 갈라지다, 금이 가다; 깨지다; n. (좁은) 틈; (갈라져 생긴) 금
If you crack a problem or a code, you solve it, especially after a lot of thought.

bite [bait] n. 한 입; 물기; 소량; v. (이빨로) 물다; 베어 물다
A bite of something, especially food, is the action of biting it.

crumb [krʌm] n. (빵·케이크의) 부스러기; 약간, 소량
Crumbs are tiny pieces that fall from bread, biscuits, or cake when you cut it or eat it.

land [lænd] v. (땅에) 떨어지다; (땅·표면에) 내려앉다, 착륙하다; n. 육지, 땅; 지역
When someone or something lands, they come down to the ground after moving through the air or falling.

sighting [sáitiŋ] n. 목격
A sighting of something, especially something unusual or unexpected is an occasion on which it is seen.

traffic [træfik] n. 차량들, 교통(량); 운항, 운행; 수송
Traffic refers to all the vehicles that are moving along the roads in a particular area.

squint [skwint] v. 눈을 가늘게 뜨고 보다; 사시이다; n. 사시; 잠깐 봄
If you squint at something, you look at it with your eyes partly closed.

grab [græb] v. (와락·단단히) 붙잡다; 급히 ∼하다; n. 와락 잡아채려고 함
If you grab something, you take it or pick it up suddenly and roughly.

magnify [mǽgnəfài] v. 확대하다; 과장하다
To magnify an object means to make it appear larger than it really is, by means of a special lens or mirror.

thoughtful [θɔ́:tfəl] a. 생각에 잠긴; 배려심 있는, 친절한 (**thoughtfully** ad. 생각에 잠겨)
If you are thoughtful, you are quiet and serious because you are thinking about something.

murder [mɔ́:rdər] n. 살인(죄), 살해; v. 살해하다, 살인하다
Murder is the deliberate and illegal killing of a person.

weapon [wépən] n. 무기, 흉기
A weapon is an object such as a gun, a knife, or a missile, which is used to kill or hurt people in a fight or a war.

‡ **incident** [ínsədənt] n. 일, 사건
An incident is something that happens, often something that is unpleasant.

Check Your Reading Speed
1분에 몇 단어를 읽는지 리딩 속도를 측정해보세요.

$$\frac{570 \text{ words}}{\text{reading time ( ) sec}} \times 60 = (\qquad) \text{ WPM}$$

Build Your Vocabulary

stroller [stróulər] n. 유모차; 산책하는 사람
A stroller is a small chair on wheels, in which a baby or small child can sit and be wheeled around.

smirk [smə:rk] n. 능글맞은 웃음; v. 히죽히죽 웃다
A smirk is a smile that expresses satisfaction or pleasure about having done something or knowing something that is not known by someone else.

fake [feik] a. 가짜의, 거짓된; 모조의; n. 모조품; v. 위조하다; ~인 척하다
A fake fur or a fake painting, for example, is a fur or painting that has been made to look valuable or genuine, usually in order to deceive people.

humor [hjú:mər] v. 비위를 맞춰 주다; n. 유머, (재치 있는) 농담
If you humor someone who is behaving strangely, you try to please them or pretend to agree with them, so that they will not become upset.

eyebrow [áibràu] n. 눈썹
Your eyebrows are the lines of hair which grow above your eyes.

buck [bʌk] n. 달러; 수사슴
A buck is a US or Australian dollar.

fluff [flʌf] n. (동물이나 새의) 솜털; 보풀; v. 망치다, 실패하다; 부풀리다
Fluff refers to any soft downy substance, especially the fur or feathers of a young mammal or bird.

hop [hap] v. 깡충깡충 뛰다; 급히 움직이다; n. 깡충깡충 뛰기
When birds and some small animals hop, they move along by jumping on both feet.

stuff [stʌf] v. 채워 넣다; (재빨리·되는대로) 쑤셔 넣다; n. 것, 물건, 물질; 일
(stuffed animal n. 봉제 인형)
If you stuff a container or space with something, you fill it with something or with a quantity of things until it is full.

droop [dru:p] v. 아래로 처지다; 풀이 죽다, (기가) 꺾이다
If something droops, it hangs or leans downward with no strength or firmness.

slap [slæp] v. 털썩 놓다; (손바닥으로) 철썩 때리다; n. 철썩 때리기, 치기
If you slap something onto a surface, you put it there quickly, roughly, or carelessly.

wheel [hwi:l] n. 바퀴; (자동차 등의) 핸들; v. (바퀴 달린 것을) 밀다; 태우고 가다
The wheels of a vehicle are the circular objects which are fixed underneath it and which enable it to move along the ground.

lock [lak] v. 고정시키다; (자물쇠로) 잠그다; n. 잠금장치
If you lock something in a particular position or if it locks there, it is held or fitted firmly in that position.

arrest [ərést] n. 체포; 저지, 정지; v. 체포하다; 막다 (be under arrest idiom 체포되다)
An arrest is the action of seizing someone to take into legal custody, as by officers of the law.

amused [əmjú:zd] a. 재미있어 하는, 즐거워 하는
If you are amused by something, it makes you want to laugh or smile.

felony [féləni] n. 중죄, 흉악 범죄
In countries where the legal system distinguishes between very serious crimes and less serious ones, a felony is a very serious crime such as armed robbery.

tax [tæks] n. 세금; v. 세금을 부과하다, 과세하다
Tax is an amount of money that you have to pay to the government so that it can pay for public services.

evasion [ivéiʒən] n. 회피, 모면; 얼버무리기 (tax evasion n. 탈세)
Tax evasion is the crime of not paying the full amount of tax that you should pay.

decade [dékeid] n. 10년
A decade is a period of ten years.

multiply [mʌltəplài] v. 곱하다; 크게 증가하다; 증식하다
If you multiply one number by another, you add the first number to itself as many times as is indicated by the second number. For example 2 multiplied by 3 is equal to 6.

unfortunately [ʌnfɔ́ːrtʃənətli] ad. 불행하게도, 유감스럽게도
You can use unfortunately to introduce or refer to a statement when you consider that it is sad or disappointing, or when you want to express regret.

federal [fédərəl] a. 연방 정부의
Federal also means belonging or relating to the national government of a federal country rather than to one of the states within it.

punishable [pʌ́niʃəbl] a. (법으로) 처벌할 수 있는; 벌을 받아 마땅한
If a crime is punishable in a particular way, anyone who commits it is punished in that way.

offense [əféns] n. 위법 행위, 범죄; 모욕
An offense is a crime that breaks a particular law and requires a particular punishment.

jail [dʒeil] n. 교도소, 감옥; v. 수감하다
A jail is a place where criminals are kept in order to punish them, or where people waiting to be tried are kept.

recording [rikɔ́ːrdiŋ] n. 녹음, 녹화; 기록
A recording of something is a record, CD, tape, or video of it.

cooperate [kouápərèit] v. 협조하다; 협력하다
If you cooperate with someone, you work with them or help them for a particular purpose.

investigate [invéstəgèit] v. 수사하다, 조사하다, 살피다; 연구하다 (investigation n. 수사, 조사)
If someone, especially an official, investigates an event, situation, or claim, they try to find out what happened or what is the truth.

prison [prizn] n. 교도소, 감옥
A prison is a building where criminals are kept as punishment or where people accused of a crime are kept before their trial.

cafeteria [kæfətíəriə] n. 구내식당
A cafeteria is a restaurant where you choose your food from a counter and take it to your table after paying for it. Cafeterias are usually found in public buildings.

grin [grin] v. 활짝 웃다; n. 활짝 웃음
When you grin, you smile broadly.

hustle [hʌsl] n. 사기; 법석, 혼잡; v. (사람을 거칠게) 떠밀다; (불법적으로) 팔다
A hustle is a dishonest way of making money.

hysterical [histérikəl] a. 발작적인; 히스테리 상태의; 너무나도 웃기는
(hysterically ad. 발작적으로)
Hysterical laughter is loud and uncontrolled.

badge [bædʒ] n. (경찰 등의) 신분증; 표, 배지
A badge is a piece of metal or cloth which you wear to show that you belong to an organization or support a cause.

pat [pæt] v. 가볍게 두드리다; 쓰다듬다; n. 쓰다듬기, 토닥거리기
If you pat something or someone, you tap them lightly, usually with your hand held flat.

passenger [pǽsəndʒər] n. 승객 (passenger seat n. (자동차의) 조수석)
A passenger in a vehicle such as a bus, boat, or plane is a person who is traveling in it, but who is not driving it or working on it.

exact [igzǽkt] a. 정확한, 정밀한; 꼼꼼한, 빈틈없는 (exactly ad. 정확히, 꼭, 틀림없이)
You use not exactly to indicate that a meaning or situation is slightly different from what people think or expect.

CHAPTERS 11 & 12

1. **How did Yax first react to Judy?**
   A. He thought that she was trying to sell cookies.
   B. He thought that she was trying to sell carrots.
   C. He thought that she was trying to join his club.
   D. He thought that she was trying to arrest someone.

2. **What was surprising to Judy about the club?**
   A. The animals didn't sleep.
   B. The animals didn't shower.
   C. The animals didn't wear clothes.
   D. The animals didn't talk to each other.

3. **How did Nanga's memory compare to Yax's memory?**

    A. Yax's memory was actually better than Nanga's.

    B. Yax only remembered what he had written down.

    C. Nanga and Yax remembered the exact same things.

    D. Nanga's memory was better since she was an elephant.

4. **Why did Judy and Nick go to the DMV?**

    A. Judy needed to renew her driver's license.

    B. Judy needed to see a friend who could get them a car.

    C. Nick had a friend who could run a license plate.

    D. Nick needed to renew his driver's license.

5. **Why was Judy so frustrated at the DMV?**

    A. She had to fill out a lot of forms.

    B. She had to wait for slow sloths.

    C. She had forgotten her ID.

    D. She was too short for the counters.

Check Your Reading Speed
1분에 몇 단어를 읽는지 리딩 속도를 측정해보세요.

$$\frac{792 \text{ words}}{\text{reading time ( ) sec}} \times 60 = (\quad) \text{ WPM}$$

Build Your Vocabulary

mystic [místik] a. 신비로운; n. 신비주의자
Mystic is the same as mystical which refers to something involving spiritual powers and influencing that most people do not understand.

spring [spriŋ] n. 샘; 봄; 생기, 활기; v. (갑자기) 뛰어오르다; 휙 움직이다; 튀다
A spring is a place where water comes up through the ground.

oasis [ouéisis] n. 위안을 주는 곳; 오아시스
You can refer to a pleasant place or situation as an oasis when it is surrounded by unpleasant ones.

scent [sent] n. 향기; 냄새; v. 냄새로 찾아내다; 향기가 나다
The scent of something is the pleasant smell that it has.

incense [ínsens] ① n. 향 ② v. 몹시 화나게 하다
Incense is a substance that is burned for its sweet smell, often as part of a religious ceremony.

waft [wæft] v. (공중에서 부드럽게) 퍼지다; n. 한 줄기 냄새
If sounds or smells waft through the air, or if something such as a light wind wafts them, they move gently through the air.

meditation [mèdətéiʃən] n. 명상, 묵상
Meditation is the act of remaining in a silent and calm state for a period of time, as part of a religious training, or so that you are more able to deal with the problems of everyday life.

buzz [bʌz] v. 윙윙거리다; 부산스럽다, 활기가 넘치다; 전화를 걸다; n. 윙윙거리는 소리
If something buzzes or buzzes somewhere, it makes a long continuous sound, like the noise a bee makes when it is flying.

chant [ʧænt] v. 구호를 외치다, 연호하다; n. (연이어 외치는) 구호
If you chant something or if you chant, you repeat the same words over and over again.

tone [toun] n. 음색; 어조; 말투; (글 등의) 분위기
The tone of a sound is its particular quality.

match [mæʧ] v. 어울리다; 일치하다; 맞먹다; n. 성냥; 똑같은 것
If something such as an amount or a quality matches with another amount or quality, they are both the same or equal.

pause [pɔːz] n. (녹음기 등의) 정지 버튼; (말·행동 등의) 멈춤; v. (말·일을 하다가) 잠시 멈추다; 정지시키다
A pause button is a button or control that allows you to stop a recording for a short time.

frequent [fríːkwənt] v. (특정 장소에) 자주 다니다; a. 잦은, 빈번한
If someone frequents a particular place, they regularly go there.

establishment [istæbliʃmənt] n. 기관, 시설; 설립, 수립
An establishment is a shop, business, or organization occupying a particular building or place.

widen [waidn] v. 넓어지다; (정도·범위 등이) 커지다
If your eyes widen, they open more.

sneeze [sniːz] v. 재채기하다; n. 재채기
When you sneeze, you suddenly take in your breath and then blow it down your nose noisily without being able to stop yourself.

scatter [skǽtər] v. 황급히 흩어지다; 흩뿌리다; n. 흩뿌리기; 소수, 소량
If a group of people scatter or if you scatter them, they suddenly separate and move in different directions.

hover [hʌ́vər] v. (허공을) 맴돌다; 서성이다; 주저하다; n. 공중을 떠다님
To hover means to stay in the same position in the air without moving forward or backward.

instructor [instrʌ́ktər] n. 강사, 교사
An instructor is someone who teaches a skill such as driving or skiing.

counter [káuntər] n. (은행·상점 등의) 계산대, 판매대; 반작용, 반대; v. 반박하다
In a place such as a shop or café a counter is a long narrow table or flat surface at which customers are served.

naked [néikid] a. 벌거벗은, 아무것도 걸치지 않은; 노골적인
Someone who is naked is not wearing any clothes.

nonchalant [nànʃəláːnt] a. 차분한; 태연한, 무심한 (nonchalantly ad. 태연하게, 무심하게)
If you describe someone as nonchalant, you mean that they appear not to worry or care about things and that they seem very calm.

grin [grin] v. 활짝 웃다; n. 활짝 웃음
When you grin, you smile broadly.

pleasure [pléʒər] n. 기쁨, 즐거움
A pleasure is an activity, experience or aspect of something that you find very enjoyable or satisfying.

folk [fouk] n. (pl.) 여러분, 얘들아; (pl.) (일반적인) 사람들; a. 민속의, 전통적인; 민중의
You can use folks as a term of address when you are talking to several people.

jaw [dʒɔː] n. 턱
Your jaw is the lower part of your face below your mouth.

lounge [laundʒ] v. 느긋하게 누워 있다; n. (호텔·클럽 등의) 휴게실
If you lounge somewhere, you sit or lie there in a relaxed or lazy way.

sight [sait] n. 광경, 모습; 시야; 보기, 봄; v. 갑자기 보다
A sight is something that you see.

lean [liːn] v. 기울이다, (몸을) 숙이다; ~에 기대다; a. 군살이 없는, 호리호리한
When you lean in a particular direction, you bend your body in that direction.

shame [ʃeim] n. 수치심, 창피; 애석한 일; v. 창피스럽게 하다; 망신시키다
Shame is an uncomfortable feeling that you get when you have done something wrong or embarrassing, or when someone close to you has.

call it quits idiom ~을 그만하기로 하다
If you say that you are going to call it quits, you mean that you have decided to stop doing something or being involved in something.

determine [ditə́ːrmin] v. ~을 하기로 결정하다; 알아내다, 밝히다
(determined a. 단단히 결심한; 단호한)
If you are determined to do something, you have made a firm decision to do it and will not let anything stop you.

spirit [spírit] n. 태도, 자세; 정신, 영혼; 기분, 마음; 진정한 의미, 참뜻
People say "That's the spirit" to approve or encourage someone's positive attitude or action.

joke [dʒouk] v. 농담하다, 재미있는 이야기를 하다; 농담 삼아 말하다; n. 우스개, 농담; 웃음거리
If you joke, you tell someone something that is not true in order to amuse yourself.

courtyard [kɔ́ːrtjàːrd] n. 안뜰, 안마당
A courtyard is an open area of ground which is surrounded by buildings or walls.

dart [daːrt] v. 흘깃 쳐다보다; 쏜살같이 움직이다; (화살 등을) 쏘다; n. (작은) 화살; 쏜살같이 달림
If you dart a look at someone or something, or if your eyes dart to them, you look at them very quickly.

neutral [njúːtrəl] a. 특성 없는; 분명치 않은; 중립적인; n. (기어 위치의) 중립
If you say that something is neutral, you mean that it does not have any effect on other things because it lacks any significant qualities of its own, or it is an equal balance of two or more different qualities, amounts, or ideas.

weird [wiərd] a. 기이한, 기묘한; 기괴한, 섬뜩한
If you describe something or someone as weird, you mean that they are strange.

curious [kjúəriəs] a. 궁금한, 호기심이 많은; 별난, 특이한 (curiously ad. 신기한 듯이)
If you are curious about something, you are interested in it and want to know more about it.

newcomer [njúːkʌmər] n. 신입자, 신참자
A newcomer is a person who has recently arrived in a place, joined an organization, or started a new activity.

dude [djuːd] n. 놈, 녀석
A dude is a man.

prompt [prɑmpt] v. 유도하다; (어떤 일이 일어나도록) 하다; a. 즉각적인, 지체 없는
If you prompt someone when they stop speaking, you encourage or help them to continue.

state [steit] v. 말하다, 진술하다; n. 상태; 국가, 나라; 주(州)
If you state something, you say or write it in a formal or definite way.

dismay [disméi] n. 실망, 경악; v. 경악하게 하다, 크게 실망시키다
Dismay is a strong feeling of fear, worry, or sadness that is caused by something unpleasant and unexpected.

vest [vest] n. 조끼
A vest is a sleeveless piece of clothing with buttons which people usually wear over a shirt.

gold mine [góuld màin] n. (지식 등의) 보고(寶庫); 금광
If you describe something such as a business or idea as a gold mine, you mean that it produces large profits.

scramble [skræmbl] v. 허둥지둥 해내다; 재빨리 움직이다; n. (힘들게) 기어가기; 서로 밀치기
If you scramble to do something or get something, you hurry or try very hard to do it or get it, often competing with other people.

license [láisəns] n. 면허(증); 자유, 방종; v. (공적으로) 허가하다
A license is an official document which gives you permission to do, use, or own something.

plate [pleit] n. (자동차) 번호판; 접시, 그릇; 판 (license plate n. (자동차) 번호판)
A license plate is a sign on the front and back of a vehicle that shows its license number.

trap [træp] n. 덫, 올가미; 함정; v. (위험한 장소·궁지에) 가두다; (함정으로) 몰아넣다
A trap is a device which is placed somewhere or a hole which is dug somewhere in order to catch animals or birds.

square [skwɛər] n. (시가지의) 한 구획; 가구; 광장; 정사각형; 제곱; a. 정사각형 모양의; 직각의
In a town or city, a square is a flat open place, often in the shape of a square.

smug [smʌg] a. 의기양양한, 우쭐해 하는 (smugly ad. 잘난 체하며)
If you say that someone is smug, you are criticizing the fact they seem very pleased with how good, clever, or lucky they are.

have a ball idiom 신나게 즐기다
If you have a ball, you enjoy yourself very much.

clue [klu:] n. (범행의) 단서; 실마리
A clue is an object or piece of information that helps someone solve a crime.

seeing as how idiom ~인 것으로 보아
You can use seeing as how or seeing that to introduce a reason for what you are saying.

moron [mɔ́:rɑn] n. 바보 천치, 멍청이
If you refer to someone as a moron, you think that they are very stupid.

bid [bid] v. (인사를) 하다, (작별을) 고하다; 값을 부르다; n. 가격 제시; 응찰
If you bid someone farewell, you say goodbye to them.

adieu [ədjú:] n. 작별(인사); int. 안녕, 잘 가
Adieu means the same as goodbye.

swipe [swaip] v. ~을 훔치다; 후려치다; n. 후려치기, 휘두르기
If you swipe something, you steal it quickly.

gosh [gaʃ] int. (놀람·기쁨을 나타내어) 어머!, 뭐라고!
Some people say 'Gosh' when they are surprised.

be up to idiom ~할 수 있다; (특히 나쁜 짓을) 하고 있다
If you are up to do something, you are able to do it or deal with it.

on the hook idiom (상황 등에) 묶여; 곤란한 입장에 놓여
If you are on the hook, you are caught in a difficult or dangerous situation.

stare [stɛər] v. 빤히 쳐다보다, 응시하다; n. 빤히 쳐다보기, 응시
If you stare at someone or something, you look at them for a long time.

pal [pæl] n. 친구; 이봐
Your pals are your friends.

Check Your Reading Speed

1분에 몇 단어를 읽는지 리딩 속도를 측정해보세요.

$$\frac{666 \text{ words}}{\text{reading time (\quad) sec}} \times 60 = (\qquad) \text{ WPM}$$

Build Your Vocabulary

vehicle [ví:ikl] n. 차량, 운송 수단; 수단, 매개체
A vehicle is a machine such as a car, bus, or truck which has an engine and is used to carry people from place to place.

exclaim [ikskléim] v. 소리치다, 외치다
If you exclaim, you cry out suddenly in surprise, strong emotion, or pain.

notice [nóutis] v. 알아채다, 인지하다; 주의하다; n. 신경씀, 주목, 알아챔
If you notice something or someone, you become aware of them.

innocent [ínəsənt] a. 순진한; 무죄인, 결백한; 무고한; 악의 없는 (innocently ad. 천진난만하게)
If you say that someone does or says something innocently, you mean that they are pretending not to know something about a situation.

counter [káuntər] n. (은행·상점 등의) 계산대, 판매대; 반작용, 반대; v. 반박하다
In a place such as a shop or café a counter is a long narrow table or flat surface at which customers are served.

dash [dæʃ] n. 단거리 경주; 돌진, 질주; v. (급히) 서둘러 가다; 내동댕이치다
A dash is a race over a short distance.

buddy [bʌ́di] n. 친구
A buddy is a close friend, usually a male friend of a man.

beat [bi:t] n. 고동, 맥박; 리듬; v. (게임·시합에서) 이기다; 때리다; 피하다
A beat is a regular movement or sound, especially that made by your heart.

hang in there idiom 버티다, 견뎌내다
If you tell someone to hang in there or to hang on in there, you are encouraging them to keep trying to do something and not to give up even though it might be difficult.

plate [pleit] n. (자동차) 번호판; 접시, 그릇; 판
On a road vehicle, the plates are the panels at the front and back which display the license number.

license [láisəns] n. 면허(증); 자유, 방종; v. (공적으로) 허가하다
A license is an official document which gives you permission to do, use, or own something.

punch [pʌntʃ] v. (자판·번호판 등을) 치다; 주먹으로 치다; n. 주먹으로 한 대 침
If you punch something such as the buttons on a keyboard, you touch them in order to store information on a machine such as a computer or to give the machine a command to do something.

digit [dídʒit] n. 숫자; 손가락, 발가락
A digit is a written symbol for any of the ten numbers from 0 to 9.

joke [dʒouk] n. 우스개, 농담; 웃음거리; v. 농담하다, 재미있는 이야기를 하다; 농담 삼아 말하다
A joke is something that is said or done to make you laugh, for example a funny story.

yell [jel] v. 고함치다, 소리 지르다; n. 고함, 외침
If you yell, you shout loudly, usually because you are excited, angry, or in pain.

hump [hʌmp] n. (낙타 등의) 혹; 툭 솟아 오른 곳 (humped a. 혹이 있는)
A camel's hump is the large lump on its back.

pregnant [prégnənt] a. 임신한
If a woman or female animal is pregnant, she has a baby or babies developing in her body.

creep [kriːp] v. (crept-crept) 천천히 움직이다; 기다; n. 너무 싫은 사람
If something creeps somewhere, it moves very slowly.

impatient [impéiʃənt] a. 짜증난, 안달하는; 어서 ~하고 싶어 하는 (impatience n. 조급, 성급함)
If you are impatient, you are annoyed because you have to wait too long for something.

frustrate [frʌ́streit] v. 좌절감을 주다, 불만스럽게 하다; 방해하다
(frustrated a. 좌절감을 느끼는, 불만스러워 하는)
If something frustrates you, it upsets or angers you because you are unable to do anything about the problems it creates.

lose one's mind idiom 미치다, 실성하다
If you say that someone is losing their mind, you mean that they are becoming mad.

spit [spit] v. (spat–spat) (탁탁거리며) 뱉다; (침·음식 등을) 뱉다; n. 침; 뱉기
To spit or spit out means to make a series of quick loud noises, especially when forcing small pieces of something into the air.

frantic [fræntik] a. 정신없이 서두는; (두려움·걱정으로) 제정신이 아닌
(frantically ad. 미친 듯이)
If an activity is frantic, things are done quickly and in an energetic but disorganized way, because there is very little time.

printout [príntàut] n. 인쇄물
A printout is a piece of paper on which information from a computer or similar device has been printed.

register [rédʒistər] v. (이름을) 등록하다; 알아채다, 기억하다; n. 기록부, 명부
If you register something, such as the name of a person who has just died or information about something you own, you have these facts recorded on an official list.

limo [límou] n. (= limousine) 리무진, 대형 승용차
A limo is the same as a limousine which is a large and very comfortable car. Limousines are usually driven by a chauffeur and are used by very rich or important people.

awe [ɔː] n. 경외감, 외경심; v. 경외심을 갖게 하다
Awe is the feeling of respect and amazement that you have when you are faced with something wonderful and often rather frightening.

run out of idiom ～을 다 써버리다; ～이 없어지다
If you run out of time, you do not have enough hours available to finish something you are trying to do.

CHAPTERS 13 & 14

1. **How did Judy justify getting into the Limo-Service area without a warrant?**
   A. She saw the limousine with the matching license plate number.
   B. She knew that she wasn't a real cop and didn't need a warrant.
   C. She noticed that the business was closed, but the gate was still open.
   D. She tossed the pen in and had probable cause after Nick tried to get it.

2. **Why did Judy and Nick know that Emmitt Otterton had been in the limousine?**
   A. They saw him on a video.
   B. They found his wallet on the floor.
   C. They asked someone working there.
   D. They found his band's CDs in the car.

3. Why did Nick want to get out of the car so quickly?

A. It was refrigerated and really cold.

B. Nick heard someone coming toward the car.

C. Nick realized that the car belonged to Mr. Big.

D. Nick saw a polar bear and was frightened.

4. Why was Mr. Big angry at Nick?

A. Nick had broken his daughter's heart.

B. Nick had sold him a skunk-butt rug.

C. Nick had stolen one of his limousines.

D. Nick had sold him a pawpsicle that made him sick.

5. How did Judy and Nick avoid getting iced by Mr. Big?

A. Judy had saved Mr. Big's daughter's life.

B. Judy was Mr. Big's daughter's best friend.

C. Nick promised to find Mr. Big a better rug.

D. Nick promised to help Mr. Big find missing animals.

Check Your Reading Speed
1분에 몇 단어를 읽는지 리딩 속도를 측정해보세요.

$$\frac{834 \text{ words}}{\text{reading time (} \quad \text{) sec}} \times 60 = (\qquad) \text{ WPM}$$

Build Your Vocabulary

frigid [frídʒid] a. 몹시 추운; 냉랭한
Frigid means extremely cold.

limo [límou] n. (= limousine) 리무진, 대형 승용차
A limo is the same as a limousine which is a large and very comfortable car. Limousines are usually driven by a chauffeur and are used by very rich or important people.

lock [lak] v. (자물쇠로) 잠그다; 고정시키다; n. 잠금장치
(lock up idiom 문단속을 하다; 철창 안에 가두다)
To lock up means to make a building safe by locking the doors and windows.

gesture [dʒésʧər] v. (손·머리 등으로) 가리키다; 몸짓을 하다; n. 몸짓; (감정·의도의) 표시
If you gesture, you use movements of your hands or head in order to tell someone something or draw their attention to something.

bet [bet] v. (~이) 틀림없다; (내기 등에) 돈을 걸다; n. 내기; 짐작, 추측
You use expressions such as 'I bet,' 'I'll bet,' and 'you can bet' to indicate that you are sure something is true.

warrant [wɔ́ːrənt] n. (체포·수색 등을 허락하는) 영장; 보증서; 근거; v. 정당하게 하다
A warrant is a legal document that allows someone to do something, especially one that is signed by a judge or magistrate and gives the police permission to arrest someone or search their house.

bummer [bʌ́mər] n. 실망(스러운 일)
If you say that something is a bummer, you mean that it is unpleasant or annoying.

waste [weist] v. 낭비하다; 헛되이 쓰다; n. 낭비, 허비; (pl.) 쓰레기, 폐기물
If you waste something such as time, money, or energy, you use too much of it doing something that is not important or necessary, or is unlikely to succeed.

on purpose idiom 고의로, 일부러
If you do something on purpose, you do it intentionally.

fake [feik] a. 가짜의, 거짓된; 모조의; n. 모조품; v. 위조하다; ~인 척하다
A fake fur or a fake painting, for example, is a fur or painting that has been made to look valuable or genuine, usually in order to deceive people.

impede [impíːd] v. (진행을) 지연시키다, 방해하다
If you impede someone or something, you make their movement, development, or progress difficult.

investigate [invéstəgèit] v. 수사하다, 조사하다, 살피다; 연구하다 (investigation n. 수사, 조사)
If someone, especially an official, investigates an event, situation, or claim, they try to find out what happened or what is the truth.

cop [kap] n. 경찰관
A cop is a policeman or policewoman.

get to idiom ~를 괴롭히다, 영향을 미치다
If someone or something gets to you, they begin to annoy, anger, upset or affect you, even though you try not to let them.

miserable [mízərəbl] a. 우울하게 하는; 비참한; 보잘것없는
If you describe a place or situation as miserable, you mean that it makes you feel unhappy or depressed.

sans [sænz] prep. ~없이, ~없는
Sans means without.

sigh [sai] v. 한숨을 쉬다, 한숨짓다; 탄식하듯 말하다; n. 한숨
When you sigh, you let out a deep breath, as a way of expressing feelings such as disappointment, tiredness, or pleasure.

defeat [difíːt] v. 좌절시키다; 패배시키다, 물리치다; 이해가 안 되다; n. 패배
If a task or a problem defeats you, it is so difficult that you cannot do it or solve it.

puzzle [pʌzl] v. 어리둥절하게 하다; n. 퍼즐; 수수께끼 (puzzled a. 어리둥절해하는, 얼떨떨한)
Someone who is puzzled is confused because they do not understand something.

sore [sɔːr] a. 화가 난, 감정이 상한; 아픈, 따가운 (sore loser n. 패배를 인정할 줄 모르는 사람)
If you are sore about something, you are angry and upset about it.

loser [lúːzər] n. 실패자, 패배자; (경쟁에서) 패자
If you refer to someone as a loser, you have a low opinion of them because you think they are always unsuccessful.

officer [ɔ́ːfisər] n. 순경; 경찰관; 장교
Members of the police force can be referred to as officers.

fluff [flʌf] n. (동물이나 새의) 솜털; 보풀; v. 망치다, 실패하다; 부풀리다
Fluff refers to any soft downy substance, especially the fur or feathers of a young mammal or bird.

beat [biːt] v. (게임·시합에서) 이기다; 때리다; 피하다; n. 고동, 맥박; 리듬
If you intend to do something but someone beats you to it, they do it before you do.

probable [prábəbl] a. 있을 것 같은, 개연성 있는
If you say that something is probable, you mean that it is likely to be true or likely to happen.

shifty [ʃífti] a. 구린 데가 있는 것 같은
Someone who looks shifty gives the impression of being dishonest.

lowlife [lóulaif] n. 범죄자; 비열한 사람; 밑바닥 생활
People sometimes use lowlife to refer in a disapproving way to people who are involved in criminal, dishonest, or immoral activities, or to these activities.

whistle [hwisl] v. 휘파람을 불다; 기적을 울리다; n. (기차·배 등의) 기적, 경적; 휘파람 (소리)
When you whistle or when you whistle a tune, you make a series of musical notes by forcing your breath out between your lips, or your teeth.

merry [méri] a. 즐거운, 명랑한
If you describe someone's character or behavior as merry, you mean that they are happy and cheerful.

tune [tjuːn] n. 곡, 곡조, 선율; v. (악기의) 음을 맞추다; (기계를) 정비하다
A tune is a series of musical notes that is pleasant and easy to remember.

annoyed [ənɔ́id] a. 짜증이 난, 약이 오른
If you are annoyed, you are fairly angry about something.

morsel [mɔ́ːrsəl] n. 소량, 조각, 조금
A morsel is a very small amount of something, especially a very small piece of food.

respect [rispékt] n. 존경(심), 경의; 존중, 정중; v. 존경하다; 존중하다
If you have respect for someone, you have a good opinion of them.

trick [trik] n. 속임수; 비결, 요령; v. 속이다, 속임수를 쓰다
A trick is an action that is intended to deceive someone.

parking lot [páːrkiŋ lat] n. 주차장
A parking lot is an area of ground where people can leave their cars.

wipe [waip] v. (먼지·물기 등을) 닦다; 지우다; n. (행주·걸레를 써서) 닦기
If you wipe dirt or liquid from something, you remove it, for example by using a cloth or your hand.

plate [pleit] n. (자동차) 번호판; 접시, 그릇; 판
On a road vehicle, the plates are the panels at the front and back which display the license number.

limousine [líməziːn] n. 리무진, 대형 승용차
A limousine is a large and very comfortable car. Limousines are usually driven by a chauffeur and are used by very rich or important people.

refrigerator [rifrídʒərèitər] n. 냉장고
A refrigerator is a large container which is kept cool inside, usually by electricity, so that the food and drink in it stays fresh.

evidence [évədəns] n. 증거, 흔적; v. 증언하다; 증거가 되다
Evidence is anything that you see, experience, read, or are told that causes you to believe that something is true or has really happened.

tweezers [twíːzərz] n. 핀셋, 족집게
Tweezers are a small tool that you use for tasks such as picking up small objects or pulling out hairs. Tweezers consist of two strips of metal or plastic joined together at one end.

snoop [snuːp] v. 기웃거리다, 염탐하다; n. 염탐꾼; 염탐
If someone snoops around a place, they secretly look around it in order to find out things.

chilly [ʧíli] a. 쌀쌀한, 추운; 냉랭한, 쌀쌀맞은
Something that is chilly is unpleasantly cold.

fur [fəːr] n. (동물의) 털; 모피
Fur is the thick and usually soft hair that grows on the bodies of many mammals.

whirl [hwəːrl] v. 빙그르르 돌다; (마음·생각 등이) 혼란스럽다; n. 빙빙 돌기
If something or someone whirls around or if you whirl them around, they move around or turn around very quickly.

compartment [kəmpáːrtmənt] n. (물건 보관용) 칸; 객실
(glove compartment n. (자동차 앞좌석 앞에 있는) 사물함)
The glove compartment in a car is a small cupboard or shelf below the front windscreen.

velvety [vélviti] a. (목소리 등이) 부드러운; (촉감이) 매끄러운
If you describe something as velvety, you mean that it is smooth and soft to sight or hearing or touch or taste.

pipe [paip] n. (pl.) (사람의) 노랫소리; 관; 피리; v. 관으로 수송하다; 높은 소리로 말하다
You can use pipes to refer to the vocal cords or the voice, especially as used in singing.

roll one's eyes idiom 눈을 굴리다
If you roll your eyes or if your eyes roll, they move round and upward. People sometimes roll their eyes when they are frightened, bored, or annoyed.

clue [kluː] n. (범행의) 단서; 실마리
A clue is an object or piece of information that helps someone solve a crime.

partition [paːrtíʃən] n. 칸막이; v. 분할하다, 나누다
A partition is a wall or screen that separates one part of a room or vehicle from another.

eyebrow [áibràu] n. 눈썹
Your eyebrows are the lines of hair which grow above your eyes.

backseat [bǽksíːt] n. (차량의) 뒷자리
A backseat is a seat at the back of a vehicle.

shred [ʃred] v. (갈가리) 자르다, 찢다; n. (가늘고 작은) 조각; 아주 조금
If you shred something such as food or paper, you cut it or tear it into very small, narrow pieces.

claw [klɔː] n. (동물·새의) 발톱; v. (손톱·발톱으로) 할퀴다
The claws of a bird or animal are the thin, hard, curved nails at the end of its feet.

mark [maːrk] n. 지국; 표시; 표석, 목표물; v. 표시하다; 자국을 내다
A mark is a small area on the surface of something that is damaged, dirty, or different in some way.

scrape [skreip] v. (상처가 나도록) 긁다; (돈·사람 등을) 긁어모으다; n. 긁기; 긁힌 상처
If something scrapes against something else or if someone or something scrapes something else, it rubs against it, making a noise or causing slight damage.

concern [kənsə́:rn] v. 걱정스럽게 하다; 관련되다; n. 우려, 걱정; 관심사
(concerned a. 걱정하는)
If something concerns you, it worries you.

spot [spat] v. 발견하다, 찾다, 알아채다; n. (작은) 점; (특정한) 곳
If you spot something or someone, you notice them.

license [láisəns] n. 면허(증); 자유, 방종; v. (공적으로) 허가하다
A license is an official document which gives you permission to do, use, or own
something.

floral [fló:rəl] a. 꽃의; 꽃으로 만든; 꽃무늬의
You can use floral to describe something that contains flowers or is made of flowers.

stump [stʌmp] v. 당황하게 하다; (화가 나서) 쿵쿵거리며 걷다; n. 남은 부분
If you are stumped by a question or problem, you cannot think of any solution or
answer to it.

drift [drift] v. (서서히) 이동하다; (물·공기에) 떠가다; n. 표류; 흐름
To drift somewhere means to move there slowly or gradually.

etch [etʃ] v. 뚜렷이 새기다; (얼굴에 감정을) 역력히 드러내다
If a line or pattern is etched into a surface, it is cut into the surface by means of
acid or a sharp tool. You can also say that a surface is etched with a line or pattern.

suspicious [səspíʃəs] a. 의혹을 갖는, 수상쩍어 하는; 의심스러운
(suspiciously ad. 수상쩍게; 미심쩍다는 듯이)
If you are suspicious of someone or something, you believe that they are probably
involved in a crime or some dishonest activity.

fancy [fǽnsi] a. 장식이 많은, 색깔이 화려한; 고급의; v. 생각하다, 상상하다; n. 애호가
If you describe something as fancy, you mean that it is special, unusual, or
elaborate, for example because it has a lot of decoration.

rush [rʌʃ] v. 급(속)히 움직이다; 서두르다; 재촉하다; n. 혼잡, 분주함
If you rush somewhere, you go there quickly.

scene [si:n] n. 현장; 장면; 광경; 풍경
The scene of an event is the place where it happened.

make a break idiom ~쪽으로 달아나다; 중단하다
If you make a break or make a break for something, you run to escape from a
person or thing.

sake [seik] n. 목적; 원인, 이유
If you do something for the sake of something, you do it for that purpose or in order to achieve that result. You can also say that you do it for something's sake.

yank [jæŋk] v. 홱 잡아당기다; n. 홱 잡아당기기
If you yank someone or something somewhere, you pull them there suddenly and with a lot of force.

shove [ʃʌv] v. (거칠게) 밀치다; 아무렇게나 놓다; n. 힘껏 떠밀
If you shove someone or something, you push them with a quick, violent movement.

sandwich [sǽndwiʧ] v. (억지로) 끼워 넣다, 사이에 끼우다; n. 샌드위치
If you sandwich one thing between two other things, you put it between them.

butt [bʌt] n. 엉덩이; (무기·도구의) 뭉툭한 끝 부분; v. (머리로) 들이받다
Someone's butt is their bottom.

guard [ga:rd] v. 지키다, 보호하다; 감시하다; n. 감시, 경호; 경비 요원
If you guard a place, person, or object, you stand near them in order to watch and protect them.

security [sikjúərəti] n. 보안, 경비; 경비 담당 부서; 안도감, 안심
Security refers to all the measures that are taken to protect a place, or to ensure that only people with permission enter it or leave it.

residential [rèzədénʃəl] a. 주거의; 거주에 알맞은
A residential area contains houses rather than offices or factories.

compound [kámpaund] n. (큰 건물이나 시설 등의) 구내; 복합체; a. 합성의
A compound is an enclosed area of land that is used for a particular purpose.

Check Your Reading Speed
1분에 몇 단어를 읽는지 리딩 속도를 측정해보세요.

$$\frac{712 \text{ words}}{\text{reading time (} \quad \text{) sec}} \times 60 = (\quad) \text{ WPM}$$

Build Your Vocabulary

lavish [lǽviʃ] a. 호화로운; 풍성한; 아주 후한 (lavishly ad. 사치스럽게)
If you describe something as lavish, you mean that it is very elaborate and impressive and a lot of money has been spent on it.

whisper [hwíspər] v. 속삭이다, 소곤거리다; 은밀히 말하다; n. 속삭임, 소곤거리는 소리
When you whisper, you say something very quietly, using your breath rather than your throat, so that only one person can hear you.

lumber [lʌ́mbər] v. (육중한 덩치로) 느릿느릿 움직이다; n. 목재, 재목
If someone or something lumbers from one place to another, they move there very slowly and clumsily.

frustrate [frʌ́streit] v. 좌절감을 주다, 불만스럽게 하다; 방해하다
(frustrated a. 좌절감을 느끼는, 불만스러워 하는)
If something frustrates you, it upsets or angers you because you are unable to do anything about the problems it creates.

teeny [tí:ni] a. 아주 작은
If you describe something as teeny, you are emphasizing that it is very small.

tiny [táini] a. 아주 작은
Something or someone that is tiny is extremely small.

paw [pɔ:] n. (동물의) 발; v. 발로 긁다; (함부로) 건드리다
The paws of an animal such as a cat, dog, or bear are its feet, which have claws for gripping things and soft pads for walking on.

arctic [á:rktik] a. 북극의; 극도로 추운, 극한의; n. 북극
The Arctic is the area of the world around the North Pole. It is extremely cold and there is very little light in winter and very little darkness in summer.

wrap [ræp] v. (무엇의 둘레를) 두르다; 포장하다; 둘러싸다; n. 포장지; 랩
When you wrap something such as a piece of paper or cloth round another thing, you put it around it.

misunderstanding [mìsʌndərstǽndiŋ] n. 오해, 착오; (가벼운) 언쟁
A misunderstanding is a failure to understand something properly, for example a situation or a person's remarks.

motion [móuʃən] v. (손·머리로) 몸짓을 해 보이다; n. 운동, 움직임; 동작, 몸짓
If you motion to someone, you move your hand or head as a way of telling them to do something or telling them where to go.

announce [ənáuns] v. 발표하다, 알리다; 선언하다
(unannounced a. 미리 알리지 않은, 사전 발표가 없는)
If someone arrives or does something unannounced, they do it unexpectedly and without anyone having being told about it beforehand.

raspy [rǽspi] a. (목소리가) 거친, 목이 쉰 듯한
If someone has a raspy voice, they make rough sounds as if they have a sore throat or have difficulty in breathing.

authoritative [əθɔ́:rətèitiv] a. 권위적인; 권위 있는
Someone or something that is authoritative gives an impression of power and importance and is likely to be obeyed.

tone [toun] n. 어조, 말투; (글 등의) 분위기; 음색
Someone's tone is a quality in their voice which shows what they are feeling or thinking.

chuckle [ʧʌkl] v. 킬킬 웃다; 빙그레 웃다; n. 킬킬거림; 속으로 웃기
When you chuckle, you laugh quietly.

break bread idiom 함께 식사하다
If you break bread with someone, you eat a meal with them.

frown [fraun] v. 얼굴을 찡그리다; 눈살을 찌푸리다; n. 찡그림, 찌푸림
When someone frowns, their eyebrows become drawn together, because they are annoyed or puzzled.

scratch [skræʧ] v. 긁다, 할퀴다; (가려운 데를) 긁다; n. 긁힌 상처; 긁는 소리
If you scratch yourself, you rub your fingernails against your skin because it is itching.

chin [ʧin] n. 턱
Your chin is the part of your face that is below your mouth and above your neck.

* **repay** [ripéi] v. (은혜 등을) 갚다, 보답하다; (빌린 돈을) 갚다
If you repay a favor that someone did for you, you do something for them in return.

* **generosity** [dʒènərásəti] n. 너그러움
If you refer to someone's generosity, you mean that they are generous, especially in doing or giving more than is usual or expected.

butt [bʌt] n. 엉덩이; (무기·도구의) 뭉툭한 끝 부분; v. (머리로) 들이받다
Someone's butt is their bottom.

disrespect [disrispékt] v. 무례한 짓을 하다; ~을 경멸하다; n. 무례, 결례
If you disrespect someone, you show a lack of respect toward them.

bury [béri] v. (시신을) 묻다; (땅 속에) 숨기다; (보이지 않게) 묻다
To bury a dead person means to put their body into a grave and cover it with earth.

snoop [snuːp] v. 기웃거리다, 염탐하다; n. 염탐꾼; 염탐
If someone snoops around a place, they secretly look around it in order to find out things.

costume [kástjuːm] n. 의상, 복장; 분장
An actor's or performer's costume is the set of clothes they wear while they are performing.

cut off idiom (말을) 중단시키다; ~을 차단하다
If you cut someone off, you interrupt them when they are speaking.

* **shift** [ʃift] v. 자세를 바꾸다; (장소를) 옮기다; (견해·방식을) 바꾸다; n. 변화
If you shift something or if it shifts, it moves slightly.

agitated [ǽdʒitèitid] a. 불안해하는, 동요된
If someone is agitated, they are very worried or upset, and show this in their behavior, movements, or voice.

evidence [évədəns] n. 증거, 흔적; v. 증언하다; 증거가 되다
Evidence is anything that you see, experience, read, or are told that causes you to believe that something is true or has really happened.

intimidate [intímədèit] v. (시키는 대로 하도록) 겁을 주다, 위협하다
If you intimidate someone, you deliberately make them frightened enough to do what you want them to do.

grunt [grʌnt] v. 끙 앓는 소리를 내다; (돼지가) 꿀꿀거리다; n. (사람이) 끙 하는 소리
If you grunt, you make a low sound, especially because you are annoyed or not interested in something.

squirm out of idiom (책임 등에서) 벗어나다
If you squirm out of something, you escape doing it.

freeze [fri:z] v. 얼다; (두려움 등으로 몸이) 얼어붙다; n. 동결; 한파 (freezing a. 몹시 추운)
If you say that something is freezing or freezing cold, you are emphasizing that it is very cold.

pit [pit] n. (크고 깊은) 구덩이; v. 자국을 남기다, 구멍을 남기다
A pit is a large hole that is dug in the ground.

beg [beg] v. 간청하다, 애원하다; 구걸하다
If you beg someone to do something, you ask them very anxiously or eagerly to do it.

gown [gaun] n. (여성의) 드레스; 가운, 학위복 (wedding gown n. 웨딩 드레스)
A gown is a dress, usually a long dress, which women wear on formal occasions.

pay it forward idiom 선행을 나누다; 선행을 베풀다
If you pay it forward, you commit random acts of kindness, especially to a stranger.

dumbfounded [dʌ̀mfáundid] a. (놀라서) 말문이 막힌, 어안이 벙벙한
If you are dumbfounded, you are extremely surprised by something.

CHAPTERS 15 & 16

1. How did Mr. Big know Mr. Otterton?

   A. Mr. Otterton was Mr. Big's florist.

   B. Mr. Otterton was Mr. Big's musician.

   C. Mr. Otterton was Mr. Big's baker.

   D. Mr. Otterton was Mr. Big's barber.

2. Why had Mr. Otterton not arrived to meet Mr. Big?

   A. Mr. Otterton never got into the car.

   B. Mr. Otterton went crazy in the car.

   C. Mr. Otterton was attacked inside the car.

   D. Mr. Otterton stopped somewhere to get dinner.

3. How did Mr. Manchas first appear to Judy and Nick?

A. He looked like a kitten who liked yarn.

B. He looked like an animal that scared other animals.

C. He looked like a savage animal ready to attack them.

D. He looked like a big jaguar with bruises and scratches.

4. What had Mr. Otterton been talking about while Manchas was driving?

A. He was talking about Mr. Big.

B. He was talking about predators.

C. He was talking about night howlers.

D. He was talking about flowers for the wedding.

5. How did Judy save Nick's life from Manchas when he charged at him?

A. She knocked Manchas into a tree.

B. She handcuffed his back paw.

C. She used a vine to trip him.

D. She kicked him in the face.

Check Your Reading Speed
1분에 몇 단어를 읽는지 리딩 속도를 측정해보세요.

$$\frac{660 \text{ words}}{\text{reading time ( ) sec}} \times 60 = (\quad) \text{ WPM}$$

Build Your Vocabulary

arctic [á:rktik] a. 북극의; 극도로 추운, 극한의; n. 북극
The Arctic is the area of the world around the North Pole. It is extremely cold and there is very little light in winter and very little darkness in summer.

groom [gru:m] n. (=bridegroom) 신랑; v. (동물을) 손질하다; 대비시키다
A groom is a man who is getting married.

feed [fi:d] v. (fed-fed) 밥을 먹이다; 먹이를 주다; 공급하다; n. (동물의) 먹이
If you feed a person or animal, you give them food to eat and sometimes actually put it in their mouths.

head table [hed téibl] n. (공식 만찬에서) 주빈석, 상석
A head table is the table at which the most important guests sit at a formal dinner.

florist [fló:rist] n. 꽃집 주인; 화초 재배자
A florist is a shopkeeper who arranges and sells flowers and sells house plants.

pick up idiom ~를 (차에) 태우다
If a person or a vehicle picks you up, they go somewhere to collect you, typically in their car.

rip [rip] v. (갑자기) 찢다; (재빨리·거칠게) 떼어 내다, 뜯어 내다; n. (길게) 찢어진 곳
When something rips or when you rip it, you tear it forcefully with your hands or with a tool such as a knife.

scare [skɛər] v. 겁주다, 놀라게 하다; 무서워하다; n. 불안(감); 놀람, 공포
If something scares you, it frightens or worries you.

evolve [iválv] v. 진화하다; (점진적으로) 발달하다
When animals or plants evolve, they gradually change and develop into different forms.

ZOOTOPIA

district [dístrikt] n. 지구, 지역, 구역
A district is a particular area of a town or country.

lush [lʌʃ] a. (식물·정원 등이) 무성한, 우거진; 멋진
Lush fields or gardens have a lot of very healthy grass or plants.

humid [hjúːmid] a. (대기·날씨가) 습한
You use humid to describe an atmosphere or climate that is very damp, and usually very hot.

clue [kluː] n. (범행의) 단서; 실마리
A clue is an object or piece of information that helps someone solve a crime.

pump [pʌmp] v. (펌프로) 퍼 올리다; (거세게) 솟구치다; 질문을 퍼붓다; n. 펌프
To pump a liquid or gas in a particular direction means to force it to flow in that direction using a pump.

steady [stédi] a. 꾸준한; 변함없는; 안정된; v. 흔들리지 않다, 진정되다
A steady situation continues or develops gradually without any interruptions and is not likely to change quickly.

stream [striːm] n. (액체·기체의) 줄기; 개울, 시내;
v. (액체·기체가) 줄줄 흐르다; 줄을 지어 이어지다
A stream of smoke, air, or liquid is a narrow moving mass of it.

mist [mist] n. 엷은 안개; v. 부옇게 되다; 눈물이 맺히다
Mist consists of a large number of tiny drops of water in the air, which make it difficult to see very far.

wind [waind] ① v. (도로·강 등이) 구불구불하다; 감다 (winding a. 구불구불한) ② n. 바람
If a road, river, or line of people winds in a particular direction, it goes in that direction with a lot of bends or twists in it.

canopy [kǽnəpi] n. 숲의 우거진 윗부분; (늘어뜨린) 덮개
A canopy is a layer of something that spreads out and covers an area, for example the branches and leaves that spread out at the top of trees in a forest.

steamy [stíːmi] a. 김이 자욱한; (더위가) 찌는 듯한
A steamy place has hot, wet air.

fog [fɔːg] n. 안개; 혼미, 혼란; v. 수증기가 서리다; 헷갈리게 하다
When there is fog, there are tiny drops of water in the air which form a thick cloud and make it difficult to see things.

moss [mɔːs] n. 이끼
Moss is a very small soft green plant which grows on damp soil, or on wood or stone.

knock [nak] v. (문 등을) 두드리다; 치다, 부딪치다; n. 문 두드리는 소리; 부딪침
If you knock on something such as a door or window, you hit it, usually several times, to attract someone's attention.

snoop [snuːp] v. 기웃거리다, 염탐하다; n. 염탐꾼; 염탐
If someone snoops around a place, they secretly look around it in order to find out things.

fancy [fǽnsi] n. 애호가; a. 장식이 많은, 색깔이 화려한; 고급의; v. 생각하다, 상상하다
Fancy can refer to enthusiasts for a sport or hobby, considered collectively.

talk out idiom ~을 철저히 논의하다
To talk something out means to discuss something such as a problem or plan completely in order to find a solution or an agreement.

yarn [jaːrn] n. 실; (지어낸) 긴 이야기
Yarn is thread used for knitting or making cloth.

playful [pleifl] a. 장난으로 한, 농담의; 장난기 많은 (playfully ad. 장난삼아)
A playful gesture or person is friendly or humorous.

punch [pʌntʃ] v. 주먹으로 치다; (자판·번호판 등을) 치다; n. 주먹으로 한 대 침
If you punch someone or something, you hit them hard with your fist.

idiot [ídiət] n. 바보, 멍청이
If you call someone an idiot, you are showing that you think they are very stupid or have done something very stupid.

creak [kriːk] v. 삐걱거리다; n. 삐걱거리는 소리
If something creaks, it makes a short, high-pitched sound when it moves.

crack [kræk] n. (좁은) 틈; (갈라져 생긴) 금; v. (문제나 난국을) 해결하다; 갈라지다, 금이 가다; 깨지다
If you open something such as a door, window, or curtain a crack, you open it only a small amount.

prevent [privént] v. 막다, 예방하다, 방지하다
To prevent something means to ensure that it does not happen.

beat [biːt] v. 때리다; (게임·시합에서) 이기다; 피하다; n. 고동, 맥박; 리듬
If you beat someone or something, you hit them very hard.

bruise [bru:z] n. 멍, 타박상; v. 멍이 생기다, 타박상을 입다; 의기소침하게 하다
A bruise is an injury which appears as a purple mark on your body, although the skin is not broken.

scratch [skrætʃ] n. 긁힌 상처; 긁는 소리; v. 긁다, 할퀴다; (가려운 데를) 긁다
Scratches on someone or something are small shallow cuts.

black eye [blæk ái] n. (맞아서) 멍든 눈
If someone has a black eye, they have a dark-colored bruise around their eye.

teensy [tí:nsi] a. 조그마한, 작은
If you describe something as teensy, you mean it is tiny in an informal way.

scene [si:n] n. 장면, 광경; 현장; 풍경
You can describe an event that you see, or that is broadcast or shown in a picture, as a scene of a particular kind.

haunted [hó:ntid] a. 겁에 질린; 걱정이 가득한; 귀신이 나오는
Someone who has a haunted expression looks very worried or troubled.

relive [ri:lív] v. (특히 상상 속에서) 다시 체험하다
If you relive something that has happened to you in the past, you remember it and imagine that you are experiencing it again.

savage [sǽvidʒ] n. 포악한 사람; a. 야만적인, 흉포한; (비판 등이) 맹렬한; v. 흉포하게 공격하다
If you refer to people as savages, you dislike them because you think that they do not have an advanced society and are violent.

howl [haul] v. (길게) 울다; (크고 시끄럽게) 울부짖다; n. (개·늑대 등의) 길게 짖는 소리
If an animal such as a wolf or a dog howls, it makes a long, loud, crying sound.

pick up on idiom ~을 이해하다, 알아차리다
If you pick up on something, you react to something that has happened or that you have noticed.

cue [kju:] n. 신호, 실마리, 암시; v. 신호를 주다
If you take your cue from someone or something, you do something similar in a particular situation.

persuade [pərswéid] v. 설득하다; 납득시키다
If you persuade someone to do something, you cause them to do it by giving them good reasons for doing it.

glance [glæns] v. 흘깃 보다; 대충 훑어보다; n. 흘깃 봄
If you glance at something or someone, you look at them very quickly and then look away again immediately.

impress [imprés] v. 깊은 인상을 주다, 감동을 주다 (impressed a. 감명을 받은)
If something impresses you, you feel great admiration for it.

dumb [dʌm] a. 멍청한, 바보 같은; 말을 못 하는
If you call a person dumb, you mean that they are stupid or foolish.

grunt [grʌnt] v. 끙 앓는 소리를 내다; (돼지가) 꿀꿀거리다; n. (사람이) 끙 하는 소리
When an animal grunts, it makes a low rough noise.

thud [θʌd] n. 쿵 (하고 무거운 것이 떨어지는 소리); v. 쿵 치다; 쿵쿵거리다
A thud is a dull sound, such as that which a heavy object makes when it hits something soft.

inch [inʧ] n. 조금, 약간; v. 조금씩 움직이다
An inch is a very small amount or distance.

hunch [hʌnʧ] v. (등을) 구부리다; n. 예감
If you hunch forward, you raise your shoulders, put your head down, and lean forward, often because you are cold, ill, or unhappy.

growl [graul] n. 으르렁거리는 소리; v. 으르렁거리다; 으르렁거리듯 말하다
When a dog or other animal growls, it makes a low noise in its throat, usually because it is angry.

race [reis] v. 쏜살같이 가다; 경주하다; 정신없이 돌아가다; n. 경주; 경쟁; 인종, 종족
If you race somewhere, you go there as quickly as possible.

primal [práiməl] a. 원시의, 태고의
Primal is used to describe something that relates to the origins of things or that is very basic.

predator [prédətər] n. 포식자, 포식 동물; 약탈자
A predator is an animal that kills and eats other animals.

Check Your Reading Speed

1분에 몇 단어를 읽는지 리딩 속도를 측정해보세요.

$$\frac{655 \text{ words}}{\text{reading time } (\quad) \text{ sec}} \times 60 = (\quad) \text{ WPM}$$

Build Your Vocabulary

복습 **chase** [tʃeis] v. 뒤쫓다, 추적하다; 추구하다; n. 추적, 추격; 추구함
If you chase someone, or chase after them, you run after them or follow them quickly in order to catch or reach them.

복습 **slippery** [slípəri] a. 미끄러운, 미끈거리는; 약삭빠른
Something that is slippery is smooth, wet, or oily and is therefore difficult to walk on or to hold.

make it idiom 가다; (힘든 경험 등을) 버텨 내다; 해내다
If you make it to a place, you succeed in reaching there.

복습 **yell** [jel] v. 고함치다, 소리 지르다; n. 고함, 외침
If you yell, you shout loudly, usually because you are excited, angry, or in pain.

복습 **leap** [li:p] v. (leaped/leapt–leaped/leapt) 뛰다, 뛰어오르다; (서둘러) ~하다;
n. 높이뛰기, 도약; 급증
If you leap, you jump high in the air or jump a long distance.

복습 **land** [lænd] v. (땅에) 떨어지다; (땅·표면에) 내려앉다, 착륙하다; n. 육지, 땅; 지역
When someone or something lands, they come down to the ground after moving through the air or falling.

복습 **branch** [bræntʃ] n. 나뭇가지; 지사, 분점; v. 갈라지다, 나뉘다
The branches of a tree are the parts that grow out from its trunk and have leaves, flowers, or fruit growing on them.

복습 **duck** [dʌk] v. 급히 움직이다; (머리나 몸을) 휙 수그리다; 피하다; n. [동물] 오리
If you duck, you move quickly to a place, especially in order not to be seen.

복습 **hollow** [hálou] a. (속이) 빈; 공허한; 헛된; v. 우묵하게 만들다
Something that is hollow has a space inside it, as opposed to being solid all the way through.

log [lɔːg] n. 통나무
A log is a piece of a thick branch or of the trunk of a tree that has been cut so that it can be used for fuel or for making things.

stalk [stɔːk] v. 몰래 접근하다; (화가 난 듯이) 성큼성큼 걷다; n. (식물의) 줄기
If you stalk a person or a wild animal, you follow them quietly in order to kill them, catch them, or observe them carefully.

frantic [fræntik] a. 정신없이 서두르는; (두려움·걱정으로) 제정신이 아닌 (frantically ad. 미친 듯이)
If an activity is frantic, things are done quickly and in an energetic but disorganized way, because there is very little time.

dispatch [dispǽʧ] n. 파견; 발송; 긴급 공문; v. 파견하다; 발송하다; 신속히 해치우다
Dispatch is the act of sending someone or something somewhere.

station [stéiʃən] n. (관청·시설 등의) 서(署); 역; 정거장; 방송 (프로); v. 배치하다
(police station n. 경찰서)
A police station is the local office of a police force in a particular area.

casual [kǽʒuəl] a. 태평스러운 (듯한), 무심한; 격식을 차리지 않는
(casually ad. 무심하게; 우연히)
If you are casual, you are, or you pretend to be, relaxed and not very concerned about what is happening or what you are doing.

chat [ʧæt] v. 이야기를 나누다, 수다를 떨다; n. 이야기, 대화
When people chat, they talk to each other in an informal and friendly way.

coworker [kóuwə̀ːrkər] n. 함께 일하는 사람, 동료
Your coworkers are the people you work with, especially people on the same job or project as you.

blink [bliŋk] v. (불빛이) 깜박거리다; 눈을 깜박이다; n. 눈을 깜박거림
When a light blinks, it flashes on and off.

lifetime [láiftàim] n. 일생, 생애
A lifetime is the length of time that someone is alive.

horn [hɔːrn] n. (양·소 등의) 뿔; (차량의) 경적
The horns of an animal such as a cow or deer are the hard pointed things that grow from its head.

check out idiom (흥미로운 것을) 살펴보다; ~을 확인하다
If you check someone or something out, you look at or examine a person or thing that seems interesting or attractive.

robotic [roubátik] a. 로봇 같은; 로봇식의, 자동 기계 장치로 된
Robotic is used about someone's way of speaking or looking when it seems to show no human feeling.

exclaim [ikskléim] v. 소리치다, 외치다
If you exclaim, you cry out suddenly in surprise, strong emotion, or pain.

chuckle [ʧʌkl] v. 킬킬 웃다; 빙그레 웃다; n. 킬킬거림; 속으로 웃기
When you chuckle, you laugh quietly.

notice [nóutis] v. 알아채다, 인지하다; 주의하다; n. 신경씀, 주목, 알아챔
If you notice something or someone, you become aware of them.

click [klik] v. 딸깍 하는 소리를 내다; (마우스를) 클릭하다; n. 찰칵 (하는 소리); (마우스를) 클릭함
If something clicks or if you click it, it makes a short, sharp sound.

hold on idiom 기다려, 멈춰; (~을) 계속 잡고 있다
If you say 'hold on' to someone, you ask them to wait or stop for a short time.

swipe [swaip] n. 후려치기, 휘두르기; v. ~을 훔치다; 후려치다
If you take a swipe at someone or something, you hit or try to hit them.

rip [rip] v. (재빨리·거칠게) 떼어 내다, 뜯어 내다; (갑자기) 찢다; n. (길게) 찢어진 곳
If you rip something away, you remove it quickly and forcefully.

scramble [skræmbl] v. 재빨리 움직이다; 허둥지둥 해내다; n. (힘들게) 기어가기; 서로 밀치기
If you scramble to a different place or position, you move there in a hurried, awkward way.

back up [bǽk ʌp] n. 지원, 예비
Back up consists of extra equipment, resources, or people that you can get help or support from if necessary.

racket [rǽkit] n. 시끄러운 소리, 소음; (테니스 등의) 라켓
A racket is a loud unpleasant noise.

tram [træm] n. 전차
A tram is a public transport vehicle, usually powered by electricity from wires above it, which travels along rails laid in the surface of a street.

dart [da:rt] v. 쏜살같이 움직이다; 흘긋 쳐다보다; (화살 등을) 쏘다; n. (작은) 화살; 쏜살같이 달림
If a person or animal darts somewhere, they move there suddenly and quickly.

slip [slip] v. 미끄러지다; 빠져 나가다; 슬머시 가다; n. (작은) 실수; 미끄러짐
If you slip, you accidentally slide and lose your balance.

pull away idiom (차량이) 움직이기 시작하다
When a vehicle pulls away, it begins to move.

struggle [strʌgl] v. 애쓰다; 허우적거리다; (~와) 싸우다; n. 투쟁; 싸움, 몸부림
If you struggle to do something, you try hard to do it, even though other people or things may be making it difficult for you to succeed.

regain [rigéin] v. 되찾다, 회복하다; 되돌아오다
If you regain something that you have lost, you get it back again.

footing [fútiŋ] n. 발을 디딤; (조직 등의) 기반
You refer to your footing when you are referring to your position and how securely your feet are placed on the ground.

prey [prei] n. 먹이, 사냥감; 희생자, 피해자
A creature's prey are the creatures that it hunts and eats in order to live.

buddy [bʌ́di] n. 친구
A buddy is a close friend, usually a male friend of a man.

offend [əfénd] v. 기분 상하게 하다; 불쾌하게 여겨지다; 범죄를 저지르다
If you offend someone, you say or do something rude which upsets or embarrasses them.

disrespect [dìsrispékt] v. 무례한 짓을 하다; ~을 경멸하다; n. 무례, 결례
If you disrespect someone, you show a lack of respect toward them.

charge [ʧɑ:rdʒ] v. 공격하다; 급히 가다, 달려가다; (요금·값을) 청구하다; n. 요금; 책임, 담당
If you charge toward someone or something, you move quickly and aggressively toward them.

split second [split sékənd] n. 아주 짧은 순간; 눈 깜짝할 사이
A split second is an extremely short period of time.

clank [klæŋk] n. 철거덕 (하는 소리); v. 철커덕 하는 소리가 나다
A clank is a loud, sharp sound or series of sounds, as is made by pieces of metal being struck together.

handcuff [hǽndkʌ̀f] n. 수갑; v. 수갑을 채우다
Handcuffs are two metal rings which are joined together and can be locked round someone's wrists, usually by the police during an arrest.

paw [pɔː] n. (동물의) 발, v. 발로 긁다; (함부로) 건드리다
The paws of an animal such as a cat, dog, or bear are its feet, which have claws for gripping things and soft pads for walking on.

cuff [kʌf] v. ~에 수갑을 채우다; (살짝) 치다; n. (상의나 셔츠의) 소맷동
If the police cuff someone, they put handcuffs on them.

post [poust] n. 기둥, 말뚝; (근무) 구역; 직책; v. (근무 위치에) 배치하다; (안내문 등을) 게시하다
A post is a strong upright pole made of wood or metal that is fixed into the ground.

tense [tens] a. 긴장한, 신경이 날카로운; v. 긴장하다
If you are tense, you are anxious and nervous and cannot relax.

edge [edʒ] n. 끝, 가장자리; 우위; v. 조금씩 움직이다; 테두리를 두르다
The edge of something is the place or line where it stops, or the part of it that is furthest from the middle.

walkway [wɔ́ːkwei] n. 통로, 보도
A walkway is a passage or path for people to walk along. Walkways are often raised above the ground.

grab [græb] v. (와락·단단히) 붙잡다; 급히 ~하다; n. 와락 잡아채려고 함
If you grab something, you take it or pick it up suddenly and roughly.

vine [vain] n. 덩굴식물; 포도나무
A vine is a plant that grows up or over things, especially one which produces grapes.

dangle [dǽŋgl] v. 매달리다; (무엇을 들고) 달랑거리다
If something dangles from somewhere or if you dangle it somewhere, it hangs or swings loosely.

canopy [kǽnəpi] n. 숲의 우거진 윗부분; (늘어뜨린) 덮개
A canopy is a layer of something that spreads out and covers an area, for example the branches and leaves that spread out at the top of trees in a forest.

bottomless [bátəmlis] a. 바닥이 안 보이는; 무한한
If you describe something as bottomless, you mean that it is so deep that it seems to have no bottom.

abyss [əbís] n. 심연, 깊은 구렁
An abyss is a very deep hole in the ground.

race [reis] v. 정신없이 돌아가다; 쏜살같이 가다; 경주하다; n. 경주; 경쟁; 인종, 종족
If your mind races, or if thoughts race through your mind, you think very fast about something, especially when you are in a difficult or dangerous situation.

figure out idiom ~을 이해하다, 알아내다; 계산하다, 산출하다
If you figure out someone or something, you come to understand them by thinking carefully.

let go idiom (잡고 있던 것을) 놓다; (생각·태도 등을) 버리다, 포기하다; ~를 풀어주다
If you let go of someone or something, you stop holding them.

misunderstand [mìsʌndərstǽnd] v. (misunderstood–misunderstood) 오해하다
If you misunderstand someone or something, you do not understand them properly.

count off idiom 번호를 부르다; 수를 확인하다
If people count off, they count to an agreed upon number so that they begin an activity at the same time.

swing [swiŋ] v. (전후·좌우로) 흔들다; 휙 움직이다; 방향을 바꾸다; n. 흔들기; 휘두르기
If something swings or if you swing it, it moves repeatedly backward and forward or from side to side from a fixed point.

net [net] n. 그물, 망; v. 그물로 잡다; (무엇을) 획득하다
A net is a piece of netting which is used for catching fish, insects, or animals.

snap [snæp] n. 탁 하는 소리; v. 딱 하고 움직이다; 찰깍 하고 닫히다; (감정 등이) 한 순간에 무너지다
A snap is a sudden loud sound like something breaking or closing.

plummet [plʌ́mit] v. 곤두박질치다, 급락하다
If someone or something plummets, they fall very fast toward the ground, usually from a great height.

cluster [klʌ́stər] n. 무리, 집단; v. 무리를 이루다, (소규모로) 모이다
A cluster of people or things is a small group of them close together.

tangle [tǽŋgl] v. 헝클어지다, 얽히다; n. (실·머리카락 등이) 엉킨 것; (혼란스럽게) 꼬인 상태
If something is tangled or tangles, it becomes twisted together in an untidy way.

siren [sáiərən] n. (신호·경보) 사이렌
A siren is a warning device which makes a long, loud noise.

convoy [kánvɔi] n. 호송대; v. 호송하다, 호위하다
A convoy is a group of vehicles or ships traveling together.

screech [skri:ʧ] v. 끼익 하는 소리를 내다; n. 끼익, 꽥 (하는 날카로운 소리)
If a vehicle screeches somewhere or if its tires screech, its tires make an unpleasant high-pitched noise on the road.

halt [hɔːlt] n. 멈춤, 중단; v. 멈추다, 서다; 중단시키다
If someone or something comes to a halt, they stop moving.

chief [tʃiːf] n. (단체의) 최고위자; 추장, 족장; a. 주된; (계급·직급상) 최고위자인
The chief of an organization is the person who is in charge of it.

cavalry [kǽvəlri] n. 기사
The cavalry is people who come and solve all your problems when you are in difficulties.

stare [stɛər] v. 빤히 쳐다보다, 응시하다; n. 빤히 쳐다보기, 응시
If you stare at someone or something, you look at them for a long time.

suspend [səspénd] v. 매달다, 걸다; (움직이지 않고) 떠 있다; 중단하다
If something is suspended from a high place, it is hanging from that place.

1. **How did Nick defend Judy from Chief Bogo?**
   A. He said that Judy should go back to parking duty.
   B. He said that Judy still had time left to solve the case.
   C. He said that he took responsibility for the missing animals.
   D. He said that he wanted to be her new partner in the police department.

2. **Why did Nick tell Judy about his time with the Junior Ranger Scouts?**
   A. He learned to track down missing animals in the Junior Ranger Scouts.
   B. He thought that Judy might be a good leader for the Scouts.
   C. He learned to never show that anything got to him and to not try to be anything else.

D. He thought that the Junior Ranger Scouts might be suspicious in the missing animals case.

3. How did the ride in the gondola above the city give Nick an idea to help find Manchas?
A. They could check the traffic cameras.
B. They could search the city from the gondola.
C. They could search the city from the highest point.
D. They could check for signs of damage from the gondola.

4. Why was Bellwether excited about helping Judy?
A. Bellwether was an expert of traffic safety.
B. Bellwether never got to do anything that important.
C. Bellwether thought that Judy was the most famous police officer.
D. Bellwether needed a break from doing hard work as the assistant mayor.

5. How did Judy feel about the wolves in the van?
A. She thought that the wolves were the night howlers.
B. She thought that the wolves were going to the Beaver Renaissance Faire.
C. She thought that the wolves were helping animals that turned savage.
D. She thought that the wolves were working for the Zootopia Police Department.

Check Your Reading Speed
1분에 몇 단어를 읽는지 리딩 속도를 측정해보세요.

$$\frac{839 \text{ words}}{\text{reading time ( ) sec}} \times 60 = (\qquad) \text{ WPM}$$

Build Your Vocabulary

confident [kánfədənt] a. 자신감 있는; 확신하는 (confidently ad. 자신 있게)
If a person or their manner is confident, they feel sure about their own abilities, qualities, or ideas.

cop [kap] n. 경찰관
A cop is a policeman or policewoman.

canopy [kǽnəpi] n. 숲의 우거진 윗부분; (늘어뜨린) 덮개
A canopy is a layer of something that spreads out and covers an area, for example the branches and leaves that spread out at the top of trees in a forest.

mammal [mǽməl] n. 포유동물
Mammals are animals such as humans, dogs, lions, and whales. In general, female mammals give birth to babies rather than laying eggs, and feed their young with milk.

scoff [skɔːf] v. 비웃다, 조롱하다; n. 비웃음, 조롱
If you scoff at something, you speak about it in a way that shows you think it is ridiculous or inadequate.

handcuff [hǽndkʌf] v. 수갑을 채우다; n. 수갑
If you handcuff someone, you put handcuffs around their wrists.

vanish [vǽniʃ] v. 사라지다, 없어지다; 모습을 감추다
If someone or something vanishes, they disappear suddenly or in a way that cannot be explained.

confuse [kənfjúːz] v. (사람을) 혼란시키다; 혼동하다 (confused a. 혼란스러워하는)
If you are confused, you do not know exactly what is happening or what to do.

aggressive [əgrésiv] a. 공격적인; 대단히 적극적인
An aggressive person or animal has a quality of anger and determination that makes them ready to attack other people.

ZOOTOPIA

officer [ɔ́:fisər] n. 경찰관; 수경; 장교
Members of the police force can be referred to as officers.

key [kiː] a. 가장 중요한, 핵심적인, 필수적인; n. 열쇠; 비결, 실마리
The key person or thing in a group is the most important one.

witness [wítnis] n. 목격자; 증인; v. (사건·사고를) 목격하다; 증명하다
A witness to an event such as an accident or crime is a person who saw it.

enlist [inlíst] v. (협조·참여를) 요청하다; 입대하다
If you enlist the help of someone, you persuade them to help or support you in doing something.

annoyed [ənɔ́id] a. 짜증이 난, 약이 오른
If you are annoyed, you are fairly angry about something.

badge [bædʒ] n. (경찰 등의) 신분증; 표, 배지
A badge is a piece of metal or cloth which you wear to show that you belong to an organization or support a cause.

stare [stɛər] v. 빤히 쳐다보다, 응시하다; n. 빤히 쳐다보기, 응시
If you stare at someone or something, you look at them for a long time.

outstretched [àutstrétʃt] a. 쭉 뻗은
If a part of the body of a person or animal is outstretched, it is stretched out as far as possible.

glare [glɛər] v. 노려보다; 환하다, 눈부시다; n. 노려봄; 환한 빛, 눈부심
If you glare at someone, you look at them with an angry expression on your face.

clown [klaun] n. 얼간이, 바보; 광대; v. 광대 짓을 하다
If you describe someone as a clown, you disapprove of them and have no respect for them.

vest [vest] n. 조끼
A vest is a sleeveless piece of clothing with buttons which people usually wear over a shirt.

wheel [hwiːl] n. 바퀴; (자동차 등의) 핸들; v. (바퀴 달린 것을) 밀다; 태우고 가다
The wheels of a vehicle are the circular objects which are fixed underneath it and which enable it to move along the ground.

joke [dʒouk] n. 웃음거리; 우스개, 농담; v. 농담하다, 재미있는 이야기를 하다; 농담 삼아 말하다
If you say that something or someone is a joke, you think they are ridiculous and do not deserve respect.

mobile [moubíl] n. 자동차; 휴대 전화; a. 이동하는; 움직임이 자유로운; 유동적인
A mobile can be used to refer to a vehicle in an informal way.

crack [kræk] v. (문제나 난국을) 해결하다; 갈라지다, 금이 가다; 깨지다; n. (좁은) 틈; (갈라져 생긴) 금
If you crack a problem or a code, you solve it, especially after a lot of thought.

stick up for idiom ~을 변호하다, 옹호하다; ~을 방어하다
If you stick up for someone or something, you support or defend them, especially
when they are being criticized.

technically [téknikəli] ad. 엄밀히 따지면; 기술적으로
If something is technically the case, it is the case according to a strict interpretation
of facts, laws, or rules, but may not be important or relevant in a particular situation.

exact [igzǽkt] a. 정확한, 정밀한; 꼼꼼한, 빈틈없는 (exactly ad. 정확히, 꼭, 틀림없이)
You use exactly before an amount, number, or position to emphasize that it is no
more, no less, or no different from what you are stating.

lead [li:d] ① n. 실마리, 단서; 선두, 우세; v. 안내하다, 이끌다; 이어지다 ② n. [광물] 납
A lead is a piece of information or an idea which may help people to discover the
facts in a situation where many facts are not known.

stun [stʌn] v. 어리벙벙하게 하다; 깜짝 놀라게 하다; 기절시키다
If you are stunned by something, you are extremely shocked or surprised by it and
are therefore unable to speak or do anything.

soar [sɔ:r] v. (하늘 높이) 날아오르다; (허공으로) 솟구치다; 급증하다
If something such as a bird soars into the air, it goes quickly up into the air.

get to idiom ~를 괴롭히다, 영향을 미치다
If someone or something gets to you, they begin to annoy, anger, upset or affect
you, even though you try not to let them.

emotional [imóuʃənl] a. 감정적인; 정서의, 감정의 (emotionally ad. 감정적으로)
Emotional means concerned with emotions and feelings.

unbalanced [ʌnbǽlənst] a. 마음이 어수선한; 약간 미친; 불균형한
If you describe someone as unbalanced, you mean that they appear disturbed and
upset or they seem to be slightly mad.

scrape [skreip] v. (돈·사람 등을) 긁어모으다; (상처가 나도록) 긁다; n. 긁기; 긁힌 상처
To scrape something such as an amount of money together means to obtain or
collect it with difficulty.

brand-new [brænd-njú.] a. 아주 새로운, 신상품의
A brand-new object is completely new.

uniform [júːnəfɔ̀ːrm] n. 제복, 유니폼
A uniform is a special set of clothes which some people, for example soldiers or the police, wear to work in and which some children wear at school.

fit in idiom (자연스럽게 ~와) 어울리다
To fit in means to live or work easily and naturally with a group of people.

troop [truːp] n. (스카우트 지역) 분대; 병력, 군대; v. 무리를 지어 걸어가다
A troop is an organized group of young people who are Scouts.

pack [pæk] n. (보이·걸 스카우트) 단(團); 묶음, 꾸러미; v. (짐을) 싸다; 포장하다
A pack is an organized group of children who are Boy Scouts or Girl Scouts.

scene [siːn] n. 장면, 광경; 현장; 풍경
You can describe an event that you see, or that is broadcast or shown in a picture, as a scene of a particular kind.

oath [ouθ] n. 맹세, 서약, 선서
An oath is a formal promise, especially a promise to be loyal to a person or country.

tackle [tækl] v. 달려들다; (힘든 문제·상황과) 씨름하다; n. 태클
If you tackle someone, you attack them and fight them.

muzzle [mʌzl] v. (동물에게) 입마개를 씌우다; n. (동물의) 입마개; (동물의) 주둥이 부분
If you muzzle a dog or other animal, you put a muzzle over its nose and mouth.

strap [stræp] v. 끈으로 묶다; 붕대를 감다; n. 끈, 줄, 띠
If you strap something somewhere, you fasten it there with a strap.

snout [snaut] n. (동물의) 주둥이
The snout of an animal such as a pig is its long nose.

mock [mak] v. 놀리다, 조롱하다; 무시하다; a. 거짓된, 가짜의
If someone mocks you, they show or pretend that they think you are foolish or inferior, for example by saying something funny about you, or by imitating your behavior.

taunt [tɔːnt] v. 놀리다, 비웃다, 조롱하다; n. 놀림, 비웃음, 조롱
If someone taunts you, they say unkind or insulting things to you, especially about your weaknesses or failures.

let go idiom ~를 풀어주다; (생각·태도 등을) 버리다, 포기하다; (집고 있던 것을) 놓다
If you let someone or something go, you allow them to leave or escape.

limp [limp] v. 다리를 절다, 절뚝거리다; n. 절뚝거림; a. 기운이 없는, 축 처진
If a person or animal limps, they walk with difficulty or in an uneven way because one of their legs or feet is hurt.

tear [tɛər] ① v. (tore–torn) 찢다, 뜯다; 뜯어 내다; n. 찢어진 곳 (tear to pieces idiom 갈기갈기 찢다) ② n. 눈물
If you tear something to pieces, you completely destroy it.

prod [prad] v. 재촉하다; 쿡 찌르다; n. 찌르기
If you prod someone into doing something, you remind or persuade them to do it.

shifty [ʃífti] a. 구린 데가 있는 것 같은
Someone who looks shifty gives the impression of being dishonest.

untrustworthy [ʌntrʌ́stwɔ̀:rði] a. 신뢰할 수 없는
If you say that someone is untrustworthy, you think they are unreliable and cannot be trusted.

pierce [piərs] v. 뚫다, 찌르다; (소리 등이) 날카롭게 울리다
If a sharp object pierces something, or if you pierce something with a sharp object, the object goes into it and makes a hole in it.

gaze [geiz] v. (가만히) 응시하다, 바라보다; n. 응시, (눈여겨보는) 시선
If you gaze at someone or something, you look steadily at them for a long time.

buzz [bʌz] v. 부산스럽다, 활기가 넘치다; 윙윙거리다; 전화를 걸다; n. 윙윙거리는 소리
If a place is buzzing with activity or conversation, there is a lot of activity or conversation there, especially because something important or exciting is about to happen.

traffic [trǽfik] n. 차량들, 교통(량); 운항, 운행; 수송
Traffic refers to all the vehicles that are moving along the roads in a particular area.

cheesy [ʧíːzi] a. 가식적인; 싸구려의, 저급한
If you describe something as cheesy, you mean that it is cheap, unpleasant, or insincere.

announcer [ənáunsər] n. (프로그램) 방송 진행자
An announcer is someone who introduces programs on radio or television or who reads the text of a radio or television advertisement.

jam [dʒæm] n. 교통 제증, 혼잡; 잼; v. 밀어 넣다; 움직이지 못하게 되다
A jam is the same as a traffic jam which is a long line of vehicles that cannot move forward because there is too much traffic, or because the road is blocked by something.

cam [kæm] n. 카메라
A cam is short for a camera.

urgent [ə́:rdʒənt] a. 다급한; 긴급한, 시급한 (urgently ad. 급히)
If you speak in an urgent way, you show that you are anxious for people to notice something or to do something.

shush [ʃʌʃ] int. 쉿 (조용히 해); v. 조용히 하라고 말하다
You say 'shush' when you are telling someone to be quiet.

chuck [tʃʌk] v. 가볍게 치다, 어루만지다; (아무렇게나) 던지다; ~을 그만두다
If you chuck someone or something, you touch or tap them gently.

impress [imprés] v. 깊은 인상을 주다, 감동을 주다 (impressed a. 감명을 받은)
If something impresses you, you feel great admiration for it.

sneaky [sníːki] a. 교활한, 엉큼한
If you describe someone as sneaky, you disapprove of them because they do things secretly rather than openly.

slick [slik] a. 교활한; (겉만) 번드르르한
A slick person speaks easily in a way that is likely to convince people, but is not sincere.

doubt [daut] v. 확신하지 못하다, 의심하다, 의문을 갖다; n. 의심, 의혹, 의문
If you doubt whether something is true or possible, you believe that it is probably not true or possible.

hopeful [hóupfəl] a. 희망에 찬, 기대하는; 희망적인
If you are hopeful, you are fairly confident that something that you want to happen will happen.

Check Your Reading Speed

1분에 몇 단어를 읽는지 리딩 속도를 측정해보세요.

$$\frac{775 \text{ words}}{\text{reading time (\quad) sec}} \times 60 = (\quad) \text{ WPM}$$

Build Your Vocabulary

assistant [əsístənt] a. 부(副)-, 조(助)-, 보조의; n. 조수, 보조원
Assistant is used in front of titles or jobs to indicate a slightly lower rank.

mayor [méiər] n. (시·군 등의) 시장
The mayor of a town or city is the person who has been elected to represent it for a fixed period of time or, in some places, to run its government.

struggle [strʌgl] v. 애쓰다; 허우적거리다; (~와) 싸우다; n. 투쟁; 싸움, 몸부림
If you struggle to do something, you try hard to do it, even though other people or things may be making it difficult for you to succeed.

stack [stæk] n. 무더기, 더미; v. (깔끔하게 정돈하여) 쌓다
A stack of things is a pile of them.

keep up idiom (~의 속도 등을) 따라가다
If you keep up with someone or something, you move at the same rate or speed as them.

dodge [dadʒ] v. (몸을) 재빨리 움직이다; 기피하다; n. 몸을 홱 피함
If you dodge, you move suddenly, often to avoid being hit, caught, or seen.

impatient [impéiʃənt] a. 짜증난, 안달하는; 어서 ~하고 싶어 하는
(impatiently ad. 성급하게, 조바심하며)
If you are impatient, you are annoyed because you have to wait too long for something.

folder [fóuldər] n. 서류철, 폴더
A folder is a thin piece of cardboard in which you can keep loose papers.

herd [həːrd] n. (짐승의) 떼; (한 무리의) 사람들; v. (특정 방향으로) 이동하다; (짐승을) 몰다
A herd is a large group of animals of one kind that live together.

graze [greiz] v. (소·양 등이) 풀을 뜯다; 스치다; n. (피부가) 긁힌 상처
When animals graze or are grazed, they eat the grass or other plants that are growing in a particular place.

slam [slæm] v. 쾅 닫다; 세게 밀다; n. 쾅 하고 닫기; 탕 하는 소리
If you slam a door or window or if it slams, it shuts noisily and with great force.

scatter [skǽtər] v. 흩뿌리다; 황급히 흩어지다; n. 흩뿌리기; 소수, 소량
(scattered a. 흩어진, 산재해 있는)
Scattered things are spread over an area in an untidy or irregular way.

tiny [táini] a. 아주 작은
Something or someone that is tiny is extremely small.

cramp [kræmp] v. (비좁은 곳에) 처박아 넣다; 경련을 일으키다; n. (근육의) 경련; 꺾쇠
(cramped a. 비좁은)
A cramped room or building is not big enough for the people or things in it.

janitor [dʒǽnitər] n. (건물의) 관리인, 잡역부
A janitor is a person whose job is to look after a building.

closet [klázit] n. 골방; 벽장
A closet is a very small room for storing things, especially one without windows.

traffic [trǽfik] n. 차량들, 교통(량); 운항, 운행; 수송
Traffic refers to all the vehicles that are moving along the roads in a particular area.

barely [bέərli] ad. 거의 ~아니게; 간신히, 가까스로
You use barely to say that something is only just true or only just the case.

puff [pʌf] n. 부푼 것; (담배·파이프 등을) 피우기;
v. (담배·파이프 등을) 뻐끔뻐끔 피우다; (연기·김을) 내뿜다; 숨을 헐떡거리다
A puff is a fluffy mass.

whisper [hwíspər] v. 속삭이다, 소곤거리다; 은밀히 말하다; n. 속삭임, 소곤거리는 소리
When you whisper, you say something very quietly, using your breath rather than your throat, so that only one person can hear you.

fluff [flʌf] n. (동물이나 새의) 솜털; 보풀; v. 망치다, 실패하다; 부풀리다
(fluffy a. 푹신해 보이는, 솜털 같은)
If you describe something such as a towel or a toy animal as fluffy, you mean that it is very soft.

mesmerize [mézməràiz] v. 마음을 사로잡다, 완전 넋을 빼놓다
If you are mesmerized by something, you are so interested in it or so attracted to it that you cannot think about anything else.

scold [skould] v. 아단치다, 꾸짖다
If you scold someone, you speak angrily to them because they have done something wrong.

swat [swat] v. 찰싹 때리다; n. 찰싹 때림; 강타
If you swat something such as an insect, you hit it with a quick, swinging movement, using your hand or a flat object.

district [dístrikt] n. 지구, 지역, 구역
A district is a particular area of a town or country.

pronounce [prənáuns] v. 발음하다; 표명하다, 선언하다
To pronounce a word means to say it using particular sounds.

glorified [gló:rəfàid] a. 미화시킨
You use glorified to indicate that something is less important or impressive than its name suggests.

secretary [sékrətèri] n. 비서
A secretary is a person who is employed to do office work, such as typing letters, answering phone calls, and arranging meetings.

vote [vout] n. (선거 등에서의) 표; 투표, 표결; v. 투표하다; 선출하다
The vote is the total number of votes or voters in an election, or the number of votes received or cast by a particular group.

mug [mʌg] n. (큰) 잔; 머그잔; v. 강도짓을 하다
A mug is a large deep cup with straight sides and a handle, used for hot drinks.

intercom [íntərkam] n. 내부 통화 장치, 인터콤
An intercom is a small box with a microphone which is connected to a loudspeaker in another room.

cringe [krindʒ] v. (겁이 나서) 움츠리다, 움찔하다; 민망하다
If you cringe at something, you feel embarrassed or disgusted, and perhaps show this feeling in your expression or by making a slight movement.

fart [fa:rt] n. 방귀; 지겨운 인간; v. 방귀를 뀌다
If someone farts, air is forced out of their body through their anus.

press [pres] v. 누르다; (무엇에) 바짝 대다; 꾹 밀어 넣다; n. 언론; 인쇄
If you press a button or switch, you push it with your finger in order to make a machine or device work.

boom [buːm] v. 굵은 목소리로 말하다; 쾅 하는 소리를 내다; n. 쾅 (하는 소리)
When something such as someone's voice, a cannon, or a big drum booms, it makes a loud, deep sound that lasts for several seconds.

lint [lint] n. 보풀; 붕대용 천
Lint is small unwanted threads or fibers that collect on clothes.

shush [ʃʌʃ] int. 쉿 (조용히 해); v. 조용히 하라고 말하다
You say 'shush' when you are telling someone to be quiet.

footage [fútidʒ] n. (특정한 사건을 담은) 장면
Footage of a particular event is a film of it or the part of a film which shows this event.

onscreen [ànskríːn] ad. (컴퓨터·텔레비전) 화면의
Onscreen means appearing on the screen of a television, cinema, or computer.

van [væn] n. 승합차; 밴
A van is a small or medium-sized road vehicle with one row of seats at the front and a space for carrying goods behind.

pull up idiom (차량·운전자가) 멈추다, 서다
If a vehicle or driver pulls up, they stop, especially for a short time.

skid [skid] v. 미끄러지다; n. (차량의) 미끄러짐
If a vehicle skids, it slides sideways or forward while moving, for example when you are trying to stop it suddenly on a wet road.

trap [træp] v. (위험한 장소·궁지에) 가두다; (함정으로) 몰아넣다; n. 덫, 올가미; 함정
If a person traps animals or birds, he or she catches them using traps.

net [net] n. 그물, 망; v. 그물로 잡다; (무엇을) 획득하다
A net is a piece of netting which is used for catching fish, insects, or animals.

gasp [gæsp] v. 숨이 턱 막히다, 헉 하고 숨을 쉬다; 숨을 제대로 못 쉬다; n. 헉 하는 소리를 냄
When you gasp, you take a short quick breath through your mouth, especially when you are surprised, shocked, or in pain.

bet [bet] v. (내기 등에) 돈을 걸다; (~이) 틀림없다; n. 내기; 짐작, 추측
If you bet on the result of a horse race, football game, or other event, you risk an amount of money on it in the hope of winning more money.

howl [haul] v. (길게) 울다; (크고 시끄럽게) 울부짖다; n. (개·늑대 등이) 길게 짖는 소리
If an animal such as a wolf or a dog howls, it makes a long, loud, crying sound.

squint [skwint] v. 눈을 가늘게 뜨고 보다; 사시이다; n. 사시; 잠깐 봄
If you squint at something, you look at it with your eyes partly closed.

surveillance [sərvéiləns] n. 감시
Surveillance is the careful watching of someone, especially by an organization such as the police or the army.

illegal [ilí:gəl] a. 불법적인; 비합법적인
If something is illegal, the law says that it is not allowed.

maintenance [méintənəns] n. (점검·보수하는) 유지; (수준·상태 등의) 지속
The maintenance of a building, vehicle, road, or machine is the process of keeping it in good condition by regularly checking it and repairing it when necessary.

emerge [imə́:rdʒ] v. 나오다; 모습을 드러내다; (어려움 등을) 헤쳐 나오다
To emerge means to come out from an enclosed or dark space such as a room or a vehicle, or from a position where you could not be seen.

detective [ditéktiv] n. 형사; 수사관; 탐정
A detective is a person, especially a police officer, whose occupation is to investigate and solve crimes.

dare [dɛər] v. 감히 ~하다, ~할 용기가 있다; 부추기다; n. 모험, 도전
(how dare you idiom 어떻게 감히 네가!)
You say 'how dare you' when you are very shocked and angry about something that someone has done.

mock [mak] a. 거짓된, 가짜의; v. 놀리다, 조롱하다; 무시하다
You use mock to describe something which is not real or genuine, but which is intended to be very similar to the real thing.

horror [hɔ́:rər] n. 공포, 경악; ~의 참상
Horror is a feeling of great shock, fear, and worry caused by something extremely unpleasant.

track [træk] v. 추적하다; (자취 등을 따라) 뒤쫓다; 발자국을 남기다; n. 길; 자국; (기차) 선로
To track someone or something means to follow their movements by means of a special device, such as a satellite or radar.

alley [ǽli] n. 골목, 샛길; 통로
An alley is a narrow passage or street with buildings or walls on both sides.

scary [skέəri] a. 무서운, 겁나는
Something that is scary is rather frightening.

CHAPTERS 19 & 20

1. **How did Judy and Nick sneak past the wolves into the asylum?**
   A. Judy started a howl that distracted the wolves.
   B. Judy and Nick disguised themselves as wolves.
   C. Nick tiptoed past the wolves and opened the gate for Judy.
   D. Nick knocked out one of the wolves with a piece of wood.

2. **What was Lionheart doing with the missing animals from Zootopia?**
   A. He was trying to keep them calm.
   B. He was keeping them locked up.
   C. He was keeping them under arrest for Chief Bogo.
   D. He was asking them questions about why they were acting crazy.

3. **Why was Lionheart afraid of the press finding out about the missing animals?**

    A. He worried that he might lose his job.

    B. He worried that he might be arrested.

    C. He worried that they might blame the biology of the animals.

    D. He worried that they would demand the animals be released.

4. **Why was Lionheart arrested by the ZPD?**

    A. He was arrested for doing a poor job as mayor.

    B. He was arrested for lying to the animals of Zootopia.

    C. He was arrested for helping wolves terrorize other animals.

    D. He was arrested for kidnapping and false imprisonment of animals.

5. **How Judy and Nick's friendship change after the press conference?**

    A. Judy had broken their friendship with her comments about predators.

    B. Judy had helped their friendship by sharing credit for solving the case.

    C. Judy had broken their friendship by taking all the credit for solving the case.

    D. Judy had helped their friendship by asking Nick to join the police department.

Check Your Reading Speed

1분에 몇 단어를 읽는지 리딩 속도를 측정해보세요.

$$\frac{958 \text{ words}}{\text{reading time ( ) sec}} \times 60 = (\quad) \text{ WPM}$$

Build Your Vocabulary

mysterious [mistíəriəs] a. 신비한; 이해하기 힘든, 기이한
Someone or something that is mysterious is strange and is not known about or understood.

distance [dístəns] n. 먼 곳; 거리; v. (~에) 관여하지 않다 (from a distance idiom 멀리서)
If you see something or remember something from a distance, you are a long way away from it in space or time.

van [væn] n. 승합차; 밴
A van is a small or medium-sized road vehicle with one row of seats at the front and a space for carrying goods behind.

checkpoint [ʧékpɔ̀int] n. 검문소
A checkpoint is a place where traffic is stopped so that it can be checked.

creepy [krí:pi] a. 오싹하게 하는, 으스스한; (섬뜩할 정도로) 기이한
If you say that something or someone is creepy, you mean they make you feel very nervous or frightened.

asylum [əsáiləm] n. 정신 병원, 보호 시설; 망명, 피난
An asylum is a psychiatric hospital.

perch [pəːrʧ] v. (무엇의 꼭대기나 끝에) 위치하다; n. 높은 자리
To perch somewhere means to be on the top or edge of something.

cliff [klif] n. 절벽, 낭떠러지
A cliff is a high area of land with a very steep side, especially one next to the sea.

venture [vénʧər] v. (위험을 무릅쓰고) 가다; 조심스럽게 말하다; n. (사업상의) 모험
If you venture somewhere, you go somewhere that might be dangerous.

ZOOTOPIA

sneak [sniːk] v. 살금살금 가다; 몰래 하다; a. 기습적인
If you sneak somewhere, you go there very quietly on foot, trying to avoid being seen or heard.

guard [gaːrd] v. 지키다, 보호하다; 감시하다; n. 감시, 경호; 경비 요원
If you guard a place, person, or object, you stand near them in order to watch and protect them.

station [stéiʃən] v. 배치하다; n. 역; 정거장; (관청·시설 등의) 서(署); 방송 (프로)
If soldiers or officials are stationed in a place, they are sent there to do a job or to work for a period of time.

motion [móuʃən] v. (손·머리로) 몸짓을 해 보이다; n. 운동, 움직임; 동작, 몸짓
If you motion to someone, you move your hand or head as a way of telling them to do something or telling them where to go.

tiptoe [típtòu] v. (발끝으로) 살금살금 걷다
If you tiptoe somewhere, you walk there very quietly without putting your heels on the floor when you walk.

start off idiom 움직이기 시작하다
To start off means to begin to move or travel.

sniff [snif] v. 냄새를 맡다; 코를 훌쩍이다; 콧방귀를 뀌다; n. 냄새 맡기; 콧방귀 뀌기
If you sniff something or sniff at it, you smell it by taking air in through your nose.

pick up on idiom ~을 이해하다, 알아차리다
If you pick up on something, you notice it.

scent [sent] n. 냄새; 향기; v. 냄새로 찾아내다; 향기가 나다
The scent of a person or animal is the smell that they leave and that other people sometimes follow when looking for them.

driftwood [dríftwud] n. 유목(流木)
Driftwood is wood which has been carried onto the shore by the motion of the sea or a river, or which is still floating on the water.

weapon [wépən] n. 무기, 흉기
A weapon is an object such as a gun, a knife, or a missile, which is used to kill or hurt people in a fight or a war.

distract [distrǽkt] v. (주의를) 딴 데로 돌리다, 집중이 안 되게 하다
(distraction n. (주의) 집중을 방해하는 것)
A distraction is something that turns your attention away from something you want to concentrate on.

impress [imprés] v. 깊은 인상을 주다, 감동을 주다 (impressed a. 감명을 받은)
If something impresses you, you feel great admiration for it.

scramble [skræmbl] v. 재빨리 움직이다; 허둥지둥 해내다; n. (힘들게) 기어가기; 서로 밀치기
If you scramble over rocks or up a hill, you move quickly over them or up it using your hands to help you.

slippery [slípəri] a. 미끄러운, 미끈거리는; 약삭빠른
Something that is slippery is smooth, wet, or oily and is therefore difficult to walk on or to hold.

slide [slaid] v. (slid–slid/slidden) 미끄러지다; 미끄러지듯이 움직이다; 슬며시 넣다; n. 떨어짐; 미끄러짐
When something slides somewhere or when you slide it there, it moves there smoothly over or against something.

waterfall [wɔ́:tərfɔ:l] n. 폭포
A waterfall is a place where water flows over the edge of a steep, high cliff in hills or mountains, and falls into a pool below.

spot [spat] v. 발견하다, 찾다, 알아채다; n. (작은) 점; (특정한) 곳
If you spot something or someone, you notice them.

pipe [paip] n. 관; 피리; (pl.) (사람의) 노랫소리; v. 관으로 수송하다; 높은 소리로 말하다
A pipe is a long, round, hollow object, usually made of metal or plastic, through which a liquid or gas can flow.

emerge [imə́:rdʒ] v. 나오다, 모습을 드러내다; (어려움 등을) 헤쳐 나오다
To emerge means to come out from an enclosed or dark space such as a room or a vehicle, or from a position where you could not be seen.

cavernous [kǽvərnəs] a. 동굴 같은; 휑한
A cavernous room or building is very large inside, and so it reminds you of a cave.

rusty [rʌ́sti] a. 녹슨, 녹투성이의; 예전 같지 않은
A rusty metal object such as a car or a machine is covered with rust, which is a brown substance that forms on iron or steel when it comes into contact with water.

medical [médikəl] a. 의학의, 의료의
Medical means relating to illness and injuries and to their treatment or prevention.

equipment [ikwípmənt] n. 장비, 용품; 준비, 채비
Equipment consists of the things which are used for a particular purpose, for example a hobby or job.

corridor [kɔ́:ridər] n. 복도; 통로
A corridor is a long passage in a building or train, with doors and rooms on one or both sides.

reveal [rivíːl] v. (보이지 않던 것을) 드러내 보이다; (비밀 등을) 밝히다
If you reveal something that has been out of sight, you uncover it so that people can see it.

shiny [ʃáini] a. 빛나는, 반짝거리는
Shiny things are bright and reflect light.

cautious [kɔ́:ʃəs] a. 조심스러운, 신중한 (cautiously ad. 조심스럽게)
If you describe someone's attitude or reaction as cautious, you mean that it is limited or careful.

scratch [skrætʃ] n. 긁힌 상처; 긁는 소리; v. 긁다, 할퀴다; (가려운 데를) 긁다
Scratches on someone or something are small shallow cuts.

crisscross [krískrɔ̀:s] v. 교차하다; 십자를 그리다; a. (많은 선이 교차하는) 십자형의
If a number of things crisscross an area, they cross it, and cross over each other.

claw [klɔː] n. (동물·새의) 발톱; v. (손톱·발톱으로) 할퀴다
The claws of a bird or animal are the thin, hard, curved nails at the end of its feet.

mark [maːrk] n. 자국; 표시; 표적, 목표물; v. 표시하다; 자국을 내다
A mark is a small area on the surface of something that is damaged, dirty, or different in some way.

take in idiom ~을 눈여겨보다; 이해하다
If you take in something, you notice it with your eyes.

sight [sait] n. 광경, 모습; 시야; 보기, 봄; v. 갑자기 보다
A sight is something that you see.

groove [gruːv] n. 홈; (음악의) 리듬; v. ~에 홈을 파다
A groove is a deep line cut into a surface.

scare [skɛər] v. 무서워하다; 겁주다, 놀라게 하다; n. 불안(감); 놀람, 공포
(scared a. 무서워하는, 겁먹은)
If you are scared of someone or something, you are frightened of them.

intimidate [intímədèit] v. (시키는 대로 하도록) 겁을 주다, 위협하다
(intimidated a. 겁을 내는)
Someone who feels intimidated feels frightened and lacks confidence because of the people they are with or the situation they are in.

^명^동 **growl** [graul] n. 으르렁거리는 소리; v. 으르렁거리다; 으르렁거리듯 말하다
When a dog or other animal growls, it makes a low noise in its throat, usually because it is angry.

^명^동 **interrupt** [ìntərʌ́pt] v. (말·행동을) 방해하다; 중단시키다; 차단하다
If you interrupt someone who is speaking, you say or do something that causes them to stop.

^명^동 **lock** [lak] v. (자물쇠로) 잠그다; 고정시키다; n. 잠금장치
(lock up idiom 철창 안에 가두다; 문단속을 하다)
If you lock someone up, you put them in prison or in a guarded hospital.

^명^동 **savage** [sǽvidʒ] a. 야만적인; 흉포한; (비판 등이) 맹렬한; n. 포악한 사람; v. 흉포하게 공격하다
Someone or something that is savage is extremely cruel, violent, and uncontrolled.

^명 **cell** [sel] n. 감방; (작은) 칸; (= cell phone) 휴대 전화
A cell is a small room in which a prisoner is locked.

^명^동 **yank** [jæŋk] v. 홱 잡아당기다; n. 홱 잡아당기기
If you yank someone or something somewhere, you pull them there suddenly and with a lot of force.

^명 **grip** [grip] n. 꽉 붙잡음, 움켜쥠; 통제; v. 꽉 잡다, 움켜잡다; (마음·시선을) 끌다
A grip is a firm, strong hold on something.

[·] **flashlight** [flǽʃlait] n. 손전등, 회중전등
A flashlight is a small electric light which gets its power from batteries and which you can carry in your hand.

swivel [swívəl] v. 돌리다, 회전시키다; (몸·눈·고개를) 홱 돌리다; n. 회전 고리
If something swivels or if you swivel it, it turns around a central point so that it is facing in a different direction.

^명 **dozen** [dʌzn] n. (pl.) 다수, 여러 개; 12개; 십여 개
If you refer to dozens of things or people, you are emphasizing that there are very many of them.

[·] **pace** [peis] v. 서성거리다; (일의) 속도를 유지하다; n. 속도; 걸음
If you pace a small area, you keep walking up and down it, because you are anxious or impatient.

feral [fíərəl] a. 야생의; 야성적인; 흉포한
Feral animals are wild animals that are not owned or controlled by anyone, especially ones that belong to species which are normally owned and kept by people.

screech [skri:ʧ] v. 끼익 하는 소리를 내다; n. 끼익, 꽥 (하는 날카로운 소리)
When a bird, animal, or thing screeches, it makes a loud, unpleasant, high-pitched noise.

lunge [lʌndʒ] v. 달려들다, 돌진하다; n. 돌진
If you lunge in a particular direction, you move in that direction suddenly and clumsily.

rush [rʌʃ] n. 혼잡, 분주함; v. 급(속)히 움직이다; 서두르다; 재촉하다
A rush is a situation in which you need to go somewhere or do something very quickly.

footstep [fútstep] n. 발소리; 발자국
A footstep is the sound or mark that is made by someone walking each time their foot touches the ground.

intense [inténs] a. 열정적인, 진지한; 극심한, 강렬한
If you describe a person as intense, you mean that they appear to concentrate very hard on everything that they do, and they feel and show their emotions in a very extreme way.

whip [hwip] v. 휙 빼내다; (크림 등을) 휘젓다; 격렬하게 움직이다; n. 채찍
If someone whips something out or whips it off, they take it out or take it off very quickly and suddenly.

go off the rails idiom 정도를 벗어나다
If someone goes off the rails, they start to behave in a way that other people think is unacceptable or very strange.

awful [ɔ́:fəl] a. (정도가) 대단한, 아주 심한; 끔찍한, 지독한 (awfully ad. 정말, 몹시)
You can use awful with noun groups that refer to an amount in order to emphasize how large that amount is.

biology [baiálədʒi] n. 생태; 생물학
The biology of a living thing is the way in which its body or cells behave.

cage [keidʒ] n. 우리; 새장; v. 우리에 가두다
A cage is a structure of wire or metal bars in which birds or animals are kept.

spare [spɛər] v. (불쾌한 일을) 겪지 않게 하다; (시간·돈 등을) 할애하다; a. 남는; 여분의
(spare me idiom 그만 좀 해; 말하지 마)
If you spare someone an unpleasant experience, you prevent them from suffering it.

come forward idiom (도움 등을 주겠다고) 나서다
To come forward means to offer to give help or information.

snarl [snaːrl] v. 으르렁거리다; 으르렁거리듯 말하다; n. 으르렁거림
When an animal snarls, it makes a fierce, rough sound in its throat while showing its teeth.

get ahold of idiom ~을 입수하다, ~을 잡다, ~와 연결짓다
If you get ahold of someone or something, you manage to contact, find, or get them.

startle [staːrtl] v. 깜짝 놀라게 하다; 움찔하다; n. 깜짝 놀람
If something sudden and unexpected startles you, it surprises and frightens you slightly.

security [sikjúərəti] n. 경비 담당 부서; 보안, 경비; 안도감, 안심
Security can refer to the group of people responsible for protecting a building.

sweep [swiːp] v. (무엇을 찾기 위해) 훑다; (빗자루로) 쓸다; 휩쓸고 가다; n. 쓸기, 비질하기
If you sweep a place or an area, you search that place or area for something.

alarm [əláːrm] n. 경보 장치; 자명종; 불안, 공포; v. 불안하게 하다; 경보장치를 달다
An alarm is an automatic device that warns you of danger, for example by ringing a bell.

blare [blɛər] v. (소리를) 요란하게 울리다; n. 요란한 소리
If something such as a siren or radio blares or if you blare it, it makes a loud, unpleasant noise.

swarm [swɔːrm] v. 많이 모여들다; 무리를 지어 다니다; n. (곤충의) 떼, 무리; 군중
When people swarm somewhere, they move there quickly in a large group.

declare [dikléər] v. 분명히 말하다; 선언하다, 공표하다; (소득·과세 물품 등을) 신고하다
If you declare that something is true, you say that it is true in a firm, deliberate way.

duck [dʌk] v. 급히 움직이다; (머리나 몸을) 휙 수그리다; 피하다; n. [동물] 오리
If you duck, you move quickly to a place, especially in order not to be seen.

evidence [évədəns] n. 증거, 흔적; v. 증언하다; 증거가 되다
Evidence is anything that you see, experience, read, or are told that causes you to believe that something is true or has really happened.

dive [daiv] v. (물 속으로) 뛰어들다; 급히 움직이다; 급강하하다; n. (물 속으로) 뛰어들기
If you dive into some water, you jump in head-first with your arms held straight above your head.

^복^습 **twist** [twist] v. (도로·강이) 구불구불하다; (고개·몸 등을) 돌리다; 구부리다;
n. (고개·몸 등을) 돌리기
If a road or river twists, it has a lot of sudden changes of direction in it.

cascade [kæskéid] v. 폭포처럼 흐르다; 풍성하게 늘어지다; n. 폭포처럼 쏟아지는 물
If water cascades somewhere, it pours or flows downward very fast and in large
quantities.

^복^습 **gasp** [gæsp] n. 헉 하는 소리를 냄; v. 숨이 턱 막히다. 헉 하고 숨을 쉬다; 숨을 제대로 못 쉬다
A gasp is a short quick breath of air that you take in through your mouth, especially
when you are surprised, shocked, or in pain.

riverbank [rívərbæŋk] n. 강둑, 강기슭
A riverbank is the land along the edge of a river.

^복^습 **sigh** [sai] v. 한숨을 쉬다. 한숨짓다; 탄식하듯 말하다; n. 한숨
When you sigh, you let out a deep breath, as a way of expressing feelings such as
disappointment, tiredness, or pleasure.

Check Your Reading Speed

1분에 몇 단어를 읽는지 리딩 속도를 측정해보세요.

$$\frac{899 \text{ words}}{\text{reading time ( ) sec}} \times 60 = (\quad) \text{ WPM}$$

Build Your Vocabulary

burst [bəːrst] v. (burst–burst) 불쑥 움직이다; 터지다, 파열하다; n. (갑자기) 한바탕 ~을 함; 파열
To burst into or out of a place means to enter or leave it suddenly with a lot of energy or force.

arrest [ərést] n. 체포; 저지, 정지; v. 체포하다; 막다 (be under arrest idiom 체포되다)
An arrest is the action of seizing someone to take into legal custody, as by officers of the law.

kidnap [kídnæp] v. 납치하다, 유괴하다
To kidnap someone is to take them away illegally and by force, and usually to hold them prisoner in order to demand something from their family, employer, or government.

imprison [imprízn] v. 투옥하다, 감금하다 (imprisonment n. 감금, 유폐)
If someone is imprisoned, they are locked up or kept somewhere, usually in prison as a punishment for a crime or for political opposition.

innocent [ínəsənt] a. 무죄인, 결백한; 순진한; 무고한; 악의 없는
If someone is innocent, they did not commit a crime which they have been accused of.

cuff [kʌf] v. ~에 수갑을 채우다; (살짝) 치다; n. (상의나 셔츠의) 소맷동
If the police cuff someone, they put handcuffs on them.

exclaim [ikskléim] v. 소리치다, 외치다
If you exclaim, you cry out suddenly in surprise, strong emotion, or pain.

address [ədrés] v. 연설하다; 말을 걸다; 주소를 쓰다; n. 주소; 연설
If you address a group of people, you give a speech to them.

sport [spɔːrt] v. 자랑스럽게 보이다; n. 스포츠, 운동
If you sport something, you wear or are decorated with it.

muzzle [mʌzl] n. (동물의) 입마개; (동물의) 주둥이 부분; v. (동물에게) 입마개를 씌우다
A muzzle is an object that is put over a dog's nose and mouth so that it cannot bite people or make a noise.

mammal [mǽməl] n. 포유동물
Mammals are animals such as humans, dogs, lions, and whales. In general, female mammals give birth to babies rather than laying eggs, and feed their young with milk.

recruit [rikrúːt] n. 신입 경찰; 신병; 새로운 구성원; v. 모집하다; (남을) 설득하다
A recruit is a person who has recently joined an organization or an army.

conference [kánfərəns] n. 회견; 회의, 학회 (press conference n. 기자 회견)
A press conference is a meeting held by a famous or important person in which they answer journalists' questions.

rhetorical [ritɔ́ːrikəl] a. 수사적인; 과장이 심한
A rhetorical question is one which is asked in order to make a statement rather than to get an answer.

application [æpləkéiʃən] n. 지원(서); 적용, 응용
An application for something such as a job or membership of an organization is a formal written request for it.

in case idiom (~할) 경우에 대비해서
If you do something in case or just in case a particular thing happens, you do it because that thing might happen.

gesture [dʒéstʃər] v. (손·머리 등으로) 가리키다; 몸짓을 하다; n. 몸짓; (감정·의도의) 표시
If you gesture, you use movements of your hands or head in order to tell someone something or draw their attention to something.

podium [póudiəm] n. 연단, 연설대
A podium is a small platform on which someone stands in order to give a lecture or conduct an orchestra.

click [klik] v. 딸깍 하는 소리를 내다; (마우스를) 클릭하다; n. 찰칵 (하는 소리); (마우스를) 클릭함
If something clicks or if you click it, it makes a short, sharp sound.

fill out idiom (서식을) 작성하다
If you fill something out, you complete a form by writing information on it.

salute [səlúːt] v. 경례를 하다; 경의를 표하다, 절하다; n. 거수 경례; 경의의 표시, 인사
If you salute someone, you greet them or show your respect with a formal sign. Soldiers usually salute officers by raising their right hand so that their fingers touch their forehead.

species [spíːʃiːz] n. 종(種)
A species is a class of plants or animals whose members have the same main characteristics and are able to breed with each other.

thumbs-up [θʌ́mz-ʌ́p] n. 찬성, 격려, 승인(의 표시)
A thumbs-up is a sign that you make by raising your thumb to show that you agree with someone, that you are happy with an idea or situation, or that everything is all right.

predator [prédətər] n. 포식자, 포식 동물; 약탈자
A predator is an animal that kills and eats other animals.

family [fǽməli] n. (동식물 분류상의) 과(科); 가족; a. 가족의
A family of animals or plants is a group of related species.

frown [fraun] v. 얼굴을 찡그리다; 눈살을 찌푸리다; n. 찡그림, 찌푸림
When someone frowns, their eyebrows become drawn together, because they are annoyed or puzzled.

yell [jel] v. 고함치다, 소리 지르다; n. 고함, 외침
If you yell, you shout loudly, usually because you are excited, angry, or in pain.

accurate [ǽkjurət] a. 정확한; 정밀한
An accurate statement or account gives a true or fair judgment of something.

rumble [rʌ́mbl] v. 웅웅거리는 소리를 내다; 덜커덩거리며 나아가다; n. 우르렁거리는 소리
If something rumbles, it makes a low, continuous noise.

disappointment [dìsəpɔ́intmənt] n. 실망, 낙심
Disappointment is sadness or displeasure caused by the non-fulfilment of a person's hopes or expectations.

biology [baiálədʒi] n. 생태; 생물학
The biology of a living thing is the way in which its body or cells behave.

escalate [éskəlèit] v. 증가되다, 확대하다, 악화되다
If a bad situation escalates or if someone or something escalates it, it becomes greater in size, seriousness, or intensity.

tension [ténʃən] n. 긴장 상태; 긴장, 불안; 갈등; 팽팽함
Tension is the feeling that is produced in a situation when people are anxious and do not trust each other, and when there is a possibility of sudden violence or conflict.

murmur [mə́:rmə] n. 속삭임, 소곤거림; v. 속삭이다, 소곤거리다, 중얼거리다
A murmur is something that is said which can hardly be heard.

ripple [ripl] v. (감정 등이) 파문처럼 번지다; 잔물결(모양)을 이루다; n. (감정의) 파문; 잔물결
If a feeling or sound ripples through someone or through a group of people, it spreads gradually.

biological [bàiəládʒikəl] a. 생물체의; 생물학의
Biological is used to describe processes and states that occur in the bodies and cells of living things.

component [kəmpóunənt] n. (구성) 요소, 부품
The components of something are the parts that it is made of.

elaborate [ilǽbərət] v. (더) 자세히 말하다; (계획·사상 등을) 정교하게 만들어 내다; a. 정교한
If you elaborate on something that has been said, you say more about it, or give more details.

nod [nad] v. (고개를) 끄덕이다, 까딱하다; n. (고개를) 끄덕임
If you nod, you move your head downward and upward to show that you are answering 'yes' to a question, or to show agreement, understanding, or approval.

aggressive [əgrésiv] a. 공격적인; 대단히 적극적인
An aggressive person or animal has a quality of anger and determination that makes them ready to attack other people.

instinct [ínstiŋkt] n. 본능; 직감
Instinct is the natural tendency that a person or animal has to behave or react in a particular way.

revert [rivə́:rt] v. 되돌아가다; 돌이켜보다
When people or things revert to a previous state, system, or type of behavior, they go back to it.

hubbub [hʌ́bʌb] n. 왁자지껄한 소리; 소란스러운 상황
A hubbub is a noise made by a lot of people all talking or shouting at the same time.

vigilant [vídʒələnt] a. 바짝 경계하는, 조금도 방심하지 않는
Someone who is vigilant gives careful attention to a particular problem or situation and concentrates on noticing any danger or trouble that there might be.

frenzy [frénzi] n. 광분, 광란
Frenzy or a frenzy is great excitement or wild behavior that often results from losing control of your feelings.

prevent [privént] v. 막다, 예방하다, 방지하다
To prevent something means to ensure that it does not happen.

quarantine [kwɔ́:rəntì:n] v. 격리하다; n. (동물·사람의) 격리
If people or animals are quarantined, they are stopped from having contact with other people or animals.

put an end to idiom ~을 끝내다, 그만두게 하다
To put an end to something means to cause it to stop.

usher [ʌ́ʃər] v. 안내하다; n. 안내인, 수위
If you usher someone somewhere, you show them where they should go, often by going with them.

interrupt [intərʌ́pt] v. (말·행동을) 방해하다; 중단시키다; 차단하다
If you interrupt someone who is speaking, you say or do something that causes them to stop.

sarcastic [sa:rkǽstik] a. 빈정대는, 비꼬는; 풍자적인 (sarcastically ad. 비꼬는 투로)
Someone who is sarcastic says or does the opposite of what they really mean in order to mock or insult someone.

primitive [prímətiv] a. 원시의; 원시 사회의; 초기의
Primitive means belonging to a very early period in the development of an animal or plant.

incredulous [inkrédʒuləs] a. 믿지 않는, 못 믿겠다는 듯한
(incredulously ad. 믿을 수 없다는 듯이)
If someone is incredulous, they are unable to believe something because it is very surprising or shocking.

state [steit] v. 말하다, 진술하다; n. 상태; 국가, 나라; 주(州)
If you state something, you say or write it in a formal or definite way.

repellent [ripélənt] n. 방충제; a. 역겨운, 혐오감을 주는
Insect repellent is a product containing chemicals that you spray into the air or on your body in order to keep insects away.

notice [nóutis] v. 알아채다, 인지하다; 주의하다; n. 신경씀, 주목, 알아챔
If you notice something or someone, you become aware of them.

nuts [nʌts] a. 미친, 제정신이 아닌; ~에 열광하는
If someone goes nuts, they become extremely angry or insane.

lunge [lʌndʒ] v. 달려들다, 돌진하다; n. 돌진
If you lunge in a particular direction, you move in that direction suddenly and clumsily.

bite [bait] v. (이빨로) 물다; 베어 물다; n. 물기; 한 입; 소량
If an animal or person bites you, they use their teeth to hurt or injure you.

flinch [flinʧ] v. 움찔하다, 주춤하다
If you flinch, you make a small sudden movement, especially when something surprises you or hurts you.

automatic [ɔ̀:təmǽtik] a. 무의식적인, 반사적인; 자동의 (automatically ad. 무의식적으로)
An automatic action is one that you do without thinking about it.

crumple [krʌmpl] v. 구기다; 구겨지다; 쓰러지다; (얼굴이) 일그러지다
If you crumple something such as paper or cloth, or if it crumples, it is squashed and becomes full of untidy creases and folds.

toss [tɔːs] v. (가볍게) 던지다; (고개를) 홱 쳐들다; n. 던지기
If you toss something somewhere, you throw it there lightly, often in a rather careless way.

trash [træʃ] n. 쓰레기; v. 부수다, 엉망으로 만들다; (필요 없는 것을) 버리다
Trash consists of unwanted things or waste material such as used paper, empty containers and bottles, and waste food.

CHAPTERS 21 & 22

1. How had Zootopia changed after the press conference?

   A. Zootopia became a city where only prey could live.

   B. The divide between predators and prey grew wider.

   C. The Zootopia Police Department fired all predator officers.

   D. There was less fear after the missing animals had been found.

2. Why was Clawhauser packing up his desk?

   A. He was moving away from Zootopia to a city with more predators.

   B. He was moving because he was assigned as Judy's new partner.

   C. He was moving because Judy was taking his job at the front desk.

   D. He was moving so that a predator wasn't the first face people saw when they came to the ZPD.

3. Why did Judy give her badge to Chief Bogo?

A. She had promised to give it to him earlier.

B. She had failed to find the missing animals.

C. She wanted to help the city and not tear it apart.

D. She had a new dream of being a mayor of Zootopia.

4. How was Gideon Gray working with Judy's parents?

A. He was planting crops on their farm.

B. He was a babysitter for all of their children.

C. He was a driver who delivered their produce.

D. He was a chef who used the produce from their farm.

5. Which of the following was NOT something that Judy learned about night howlers?

A. They were a name for a type of flower.

B. A bunny could go savage after eating one.

C. They were beginning to grow wild in Zootopia.

D. Her parents grew them to keep bugs off the produce.

Check Your Reading Speed
1분에 몇 단어를 읽는지 리딩 속도를 측정해보세요.

$$\frac{542 \text{ words}}{\text{reading time ( ) sec}} \times 60 = (\qquad) \text{ WPM}$$

Build Your Vocabulary

conference [kánfərəns] n. 회견; 회의, 학회 (press conference n. 기자 회견)
A press conference is a meeting held by a famous or important person in which they answer journalists' questions.

wedge [wedʒ] n. 분열의 원인; 쐐기; v. (좁은 틈 사이에) 끼워 넣다; 고정시키다
(drive a wedge idiom ~의 사이를 틀어지게 하다)
If someone drives a wedge between two people who are close, they cause ill feelings between them in order to weaken their relationship.

conflict [kənflíkt] n. 갈등, 충돌; 대립, 마찰; v. 상충하다
Conflict is fighting between countries or groups of people.

protest [próutest] n. 항의 (운동); 시위; v. 항의하다, 이의를 제기하다
A protest is the act of saying or showing publicly that you object to something.

opposing [əpóuziŋ] a. 서로 대립하는; 서로 다른
Opposing groups of people disagree about something or are in competition with one another.

prey [prei] n. 먹이, 사냥감; 희생자, 피해자
A creature's prey are the creatures that it hunts and eats in order to live.

station [stéiʃən] n. 방송 (프로); 역; 정거장; (관청·시설 등의) 서(署); v. 배치하다
If you talk about a particular radio or television station, you are referring to the programs broadcast by a particular radio or television company.

pop [pap] n. 팝(뮤직); 펑 (하고 터지는 소리); v. 급히 놓다; 펑 하는 소리가 나다; 잡다
Pop is modern music that usually has a strong rhythm and uses electronic equipment.

rally [ræli] v. (원조·지지를 위해) 단결하다; 회복되다; n. (대규모) 집회
When people rally to something or when something rallies them, they unite to support it.

ZOOTOPIA

blind [blaind] a. 맹목적인; 눈이 먼; 눈치 채지 못하는; v. 눈이 멀게 하다; 맹목적이 되게 하다
(blindly ad. 맹목적으로, 무턱대고)
If you say that someone does something blindly, you mean that they do it without having enough information, or without thinking about it.

assign [əsáin] v. ~의 탓으로 하다; (일·책임 등을) 맡기다; (사람을) 배치하다
If you assign a particular function or value to someone or something, you say they have it.

blame [bleim] n. 책임; 탓; v. ~을 탓하다, ~의 책임으로 보다
The blame for something bad that has happened is the responsibility for causing it or letting it happen.

irresponsible [ìrispánsəbl] a. 무책임한
If you describe someone as irresponsible, you are criticizing them because they do things without properly considering their possible consequences.

label [léibəl] v. 꼬리표를 붙이다; 라벨을 붙이다; (표에 정보를) 적다; n. 표, 라벨; 꼬리표
If you say that someone or something is labelled as a particular thing, you mean that people generally describe them that way and you think that this is unfair.

exhaust [igzɔ́ːst] v. 기진맥진하게 하다; 다 써 버리다; n. (자동차 등의) 배기가스
(exhausted a. 기진맥진한)
If something exhausts you, it makes you so tired, either physically or mentally, that you have no energy left.

flail [fleil] v. 마구 움직이다; (팔다리를) 마구 흔들다
If your arms or legs flail or if you flail them about, they wave about in an energetic but uncontrolled way.

pad [pæd] v. 완충재를 대다; 소리 안 나게 걷다; n. 패드; 보호대 (padded a. 속을 채워 메운)
If you pad something, you put something soft in it or over it in order to make it less hard, to protect it, or to give it a different shape.

arrive [əráiv] v. 성공하다; 명성을 얻다; 도착하다
If you have arrived, you have achieved success and become famous.

boiler [bɔ́ilər] n. 보일러
A boiler is a device which burns gas, oil, electricity, or coal in order to provide hot water, especially for the central heating in a building.

disappointment [dìsəpɔ́intmənt] n. 실망, 낙심
Disappointment is sadness or displeasure caused by the non-fulfilment of a person's hopes or expectations.

evident [évədənt] a. 분명한, 눈에 띄는
If something is evident, you notice it easily and clearly.

command [kəmǽnd] v. 명령하다, 지시하다; 지휘하다; n. 명령; 지휘, 통솔
If someone in authority commands you to do something, they tell you that you must do it.

fancy [fǽnsi] a. 고급의; 장식이 많은, 색깔이 화려한; v. 생각하다, 상상하다; n. 애호가
If you describe something as fancy, you mean that it is very expensive or of very high quality, and you often dislike it because of this.

pamphlet [pǽmflət] n. 소책자, 팸플릿
A pamphlet is a very thin book, with a paper cover, which gives information about something.

confuse [kənfjúːz] v. (사람을) 혼란시키다; 혼동하다 (confused a. 혼란스러워하는)
If you are confused, you do not know exactly what is happening or what to do.

scare [skɛər] v. 무서워하다; 겁주다, 놀라게 하다; n. 불안(감); 놀람, 공포
(scared a. 무서워하는, 겁먹은)
If you are scared of someone or something, you are frightened of them.

chief [tʃiːf] n. (단체의) 최고위자; 추장, 족장; a. 주된; (계급·직급상) 최고위자인
The chief of an organization is the person who is in charge of it.

credit [krédit] n. 인정; 칭찬; 신뢰, 신용; 입금; v. 입금하다; ~의 공으로 믿다; ~을 ~로 여기다
To give someone credit for a good quality means to believe that they have it.

cop [kap] n. 경찰관
A cop is a policeman or policewoman.

with all due respect idiom 대단히 죄송하지만
You can say with respect or with all due respect when you are politely disagreeing with someone or criticizing them.

serve [səːrv] v. (어떤 조직·국가 등을 위해) 일하다; (음식을) 제공하다; (상품·서비스를) 제공하다
If you serve your country, an organization, or a person, you do useful work for them.

tear [tɛər] ① v. 찢다, 뜯다; 뜯어 내다; n. 찢어진 곳 (tear apart idiom 분열시키다) ② n. 눈물
To tear apart means to separate people in a family, an organization, or a country and make them argue with or fight against each other.

badge [bædʒ] n. (경찰 등의) 신분증; 표, 배지

A badge is a piece of metal or cloth which you wear to show that you belong to an organization or support a cause.

deserve [dizə́ːrv] v. ~을 받을 만하다, ~을 누릴 자격이 있다; ~을 당해야 마땅하다

If you say that a person or thing deserves something, you mean that they should have it or receive it because of their actions or qualities.

Check Your Reading Speed

1분에 몇 단어를 읽는지 리딩 속도를 측정해보세요.

$$\frac{501 \text{ words}}{\text{reading time ( ) sec}} \times 60 = (\qquad) \text{ WPM}$$

Build Your Vocabulary

stand [stænd] n. 가판대, 좌판; (경기장의) 관중석; v. 서다, 서 있다; (어떤 위치에) 세우다
A stand is a small shop or stall, outdoors or in a large public building.

customer [kʌ́stəmər] n. 손님, 고객
A customer is someone who buys goods or services, especially from a shop.

dozen [dʌzn] n. 12개; (pl.) 다수, 여러 개; 십여 개
If you have a dozen things, you have twelve of them.

robotic [roubátik] a. 로봇 같은; 로봇식의, 자동 기계 장치로 된 (robotically ad. 로봇같이)
Robotic is used about someone's way of speaking or looking when it seems to show no human feeling.

concern [kənsə́:rn] v. 걱정스럽게 하다; 관련되다; n. 우려, 걱정; 관심사
(concerned a. 걱정하는)
If something concerns you, it worries you.

droopy [drú:pi] a. 축 늘어진, 수그린; 지친, 의기소침한
If you describe something as droopy, you mean that it hangs down with no strength or firmness.

innocent [ínəsənt] a. 무죄인, 결백한; 순진한; 무고한; 악의 없는
If someone is innocent, they did not commit a crime which they have been accused of.

speak of the devil idiom 호랑이도 제 말하면 온다더니
People say speak of the devil, if someone they have just been talking about appears unexpectedly.

beep [bi:p] n. 삑 (하는 소리); v. 삐 소리를 내다; (경적을) 울리다
A beep is a short, loud sound like that made by a car horn or a telephone answering machine.

horn [hɔːrn] n. (차량의) 경적; (양·소 등의) 뿔
On a vehicle such as a car, the horn is the device that makes a loud noise as a signal or warning.

blare [blɛər] v. (소리를) 요란하게 울리다; n. 요란한 소리
If something such as a siren or radio blares or if you blare it, it makes a loud, unpleasant noise.

pull up idiom (차량·운전자가) 멈추다, 서다
If a vehicle or driver pulls up, they stop, especially for a short time.

widen [waidn] v. 넓어지다; (정도·범위 등이) 커지다
If your eyes widen, they open more.

sign [sain] n. 표지판, 간판; 징후; 몸짓, 신호; v. 서명하다; 신호를 보내다
A sign is a piece of wood, metal, or plastic with words or pictures on it. Signs give you information about something, or give you a warning or an instruction.

epicurean [èpikjuəríːən] a. 식도락의, 미식가적인; 쾌락주의의
Epicurean food is of very good quality, especially unusual or rare food.

delight [diláit] n. 큰 기쁨을 주는 것; 기쁨, 즐거움; v. 많은 기쁨을 주다, 아주 즐겁게 하다
You can refer to someone or something that gives you great pleasure or enjoyment as a delight.

nod [nad] v. (고개를) 끄덕이다, 까딱하다; n. (고개를) 끄덕임
If you nod, you move your head downward and upward to show that you are answering 'yes' to a question, or to show agreement, understanding, or approval.

borough [bə́ːrou] n. 자치구
A borough is a town, or a district within a large town, which has its own council.

youth n. 어린 시절; 젊음, 청춘
Someone's youth is the period of their life during which they are a child, before they are a fully mature adult.

doubt [daut] n. 의심, 의혹, 의문; v. 확신하지 못하다, 의심하다, 의문을 갖다
(self-doubt n. 자기 회의)
Self-doubt is a lack of confidence in yourself and your abilities.

manifest [mǽnəfèst] v. (감정·태도 등을 분명히) 나타내다; 분명해지다; a. 분명한
If you manifest a particular quality, feeling, or illness, or if it manifests itself, it becomes visible or obvious.

unchecked [ʌ̀nʧékt] a. 억제되지 않은
If something harmful or undesirable is left unchecked, nobody controls it or prevents it from growing or developing.

rage [reidʒ] n. 격렬한 분노; v. 몹시 화를 내다; 맹렬히 계속되다
Rage is strong anger that is difficult to control.

aggressive [əgrésiv] a. 공격적인; 대단히 적극적인 (aggression n. 공격성)
Aggression is a quality of anger and determination that makes you ready to attack other people.

jerk [dʒə:rk] n. 얼간이; 홱 움직임; v. 홱 움직이다
If you call someone a jerk, you are insulting them because you think they are stupid or you do not like them.

know a thing or two idiom (~에 대해) 좀 알다
If you say that a person knows a thing or two about something, you mean that they know a lot about it or are good at it.

beeline [bí:làin] v. 일직선으로 나가다; n. 직선; 최단 코스
If you beeline for someone or something, you go directly and quickly toward them.

howl [haul] v. (길게) 울다; (크고 시끄럽게) 울부짖다; n. (개·늑대 등의) 길게 짖는 소리
If an animal such as a wolf or a dog howls, it makes a long, loud, crying sound.

prick up idiom 귀를 쫑긋 세우다; 귀담아 듣다
If you prick up your ears, you listen carefully to what someone is saying.

edge [edʒ] n. 끝, 가장자리; 우위; v. 조금씩 움직이다; 테두리를 두르다
The edge of something is the place or line where it stops, or the part of it that is furthest from the middle.

crop [krap] n. (농)작물; 수확량
Crops are plants such as wheat and potatoes that are grown in large quantities for food.

account [əkáunt] n. 설명, 이야기; 계좌; v. 간주하다, 여기다 (on account of idiom ~때문에)
You use on account of to introduce the reason or explanation for something.

nuts [nʌts] a. 미친, 제정신이 아닌; ~에 열광하는
If someone goes nuts, they become extremely angry or insane.

bite [bait] v. (bit-bit) (이빨로) 물다; 베어 물다; n. 물기; 한 입; 소량
If an animal or person bites you, they use their teeth to hurt or injure you.

put the pieces together idiom (사실·세부 사항들을) 종합하다
If you put the pieces together, you discover a story by putting together separate facts or pieces of evidence.

sizable [sáizəbl] a. 꽤 많은, 상당한 크기의
Sizable means fairly large.

race [reis] v. 정신없이 돌아가다; 쏜살같이 가다; 경주하다; n. 경주; 경쟁; 인종, 종족
If your mind races, or if thoughts race through your mind, you think very fast about something, especially when you are in a difficult or dangerous situation.

toss [tɔːs] v. (가볍게) 던지다; (고개를) 홱 쳐들다; n. 던지기
If you toss something somewhere, you throw it there lightly, often in a rather careless way.

peel out idiom 쌩 하고 떠나다
If you peel out, you suddenly make a car start moving very quickly so that it makes a lot of noise.

CHAPTERS 23 & 24

1. **Why did Judy think the predators were going savage?**
   A. Judy thought that it was just part of their biology.
   B. Judy thought that they were accidentally eating night howlers.
   C. Judy thought that someone was targeting predators on purpose.
   D. Judy thought that they were trying to scare prey out of Zootopia.

2. **Why did Judy go back to Nick?**
   A. She wanted to warn him to leave Zootopia.
   B. She wanted him to help her fix Zootopia.
   C. She wanted to get her carrot pen back.
   D. She wanted to begin a life of crime.

3. What was Weaselton doing when Judy and Nick found him?

A. He was selling flowers.

B. He was selling pawpsicles.

C. He was selling night howlers.

D. He was selling knock-off movies.

4. Why did Judy need to find Duke Weaselton?

A. He had stolen night howlers for a reason.

B. He had eaten a night howler and turned savage.

C. He had been a police officer but was now a criminal.

D. He had been savage before but had gotten better over time.

5. How did Judy and Nick get Weaselton to talk?

A. They brought him to Little Rodentia.

B. They brought him to Doug underground.

C. They brought him to Mr. Big and his icy pit.

D. They brought him to the Zootopia Police Department.

Check Your Reading Speed
1분에 몇 단어를 읽는지 리딩 속도를 측정해보세요.

$$\frac{322 \text{ words}}{\text{reading time ( ) sec}} \times 60 = (\qquad) \text{ WPM}$$

Build Your Vocabulary

toxic [táksik] a. 유독성의
A toxic substance is poisonous.

on purpose idiom 고의로, 일부러
If you do something on purpose, you do it intentionally.

savage [sǽvidʒ] a. 야만적인, 흉포한; (비판 등이) 맹렬한; n. 포악한 사람; v. 흉포하게 공격하다
Someone or something that is savage is extremely cruel, violent, and uncontrolled.

blame [bleim] v. ~을 탓하다, ~의 책임으로 보다; n. 책임; 탓
If you blame a person or thing for something bad, you believe or say that they are responsible for it or that they caused it.

ignorant [ígnərənt] a. 무지한, 무식한; 무지막지한
If you describe someone as ignorant, you mean that they do not know things they should know.

irresponsible [ìrispánsəbl] a. 무책임한
If you describe someone as irresponsible, you are criticizing them because they do things without properly considering their possible consequences.

small-minded [smɔ́:l-máindid] a. 속이 좁은, 좀스러운, 옹졸한
If you say that someone is small-minded, you are critical of them because they have fixed opinions and are unwilling to change them or to think about more general subjects.

sigh [sai] v. 한숨을 쉬다, 한숨짓다; 탄식하듯 말하다; n. 한숨
When you sigh, you let out a deep breath, as a way of expressing feelings such as disappointment, tiredness, or pleasure.

horrible [hɔ́:rəbl] a. 못된; 소름끼치는, 무시무시한; 지긋지긋한, 끔찍한
If you describe something or someone as horrible, you do not like them at all.

all along idiom 처음부터, 내내, 계속
If something has been true or been present all along, it has been true or been present throughout a period of time.

dumb [dʌm] a. 멍청한, 바보 같은; 말을 못 하는
If you call a person dumb, you mean that they are stupid or foolish.

awkward [ɔ́:kwərd] a. (기분이) 어색한; (처리하기) 곤란한; 불편한
(awkwardly ad. 어색하게, 서투르게)
An awkward situation is embarrassing and difficult to deal with.

emerge [imə́:rdʒ] v. 나오다, 모습을 드러내다; (어려움 등을) 헤쳐 나오다
To emerge means to come out from an enclosed or dark space such as a room or a vehicle, or from a position where you could not be seen.

cheer up idiom 힘내; 기운을 내다
You can say 'cheer up' to someone in order to tell them to try to be happier.

erase [iréis] v. (녹음테이프나 컴퓨터에서 내용을) 지우다; (지우개 등으로) 지우다
If you erase sound which has been recorded on a tape or information which has been stored in a computer, you completely remove or destroy it.

well [wel] v. (액체가) 솟아 나오다, 샘솟다; n. 우물; 근원
If liquids, for example tears, well, they come to the surface and form a pool.

emotional [imóuʃənl] a. 감정적인; 정서의, 감정의
If someone is or becomes emotional, they show their feelings very openly, especially because they are upset.

tail [teil] n. (동물의) 꼬리; 끝부분; v. 미행하다
The tail of an animal, bird, or fish is the part extending beyond the end of its body.

grab [græb] v. (와락·단단히) 붙잡다; 급히 ~하다; n. 와락 잡아채려고 함
If you grab something, you take it or pick it up suddenly and roughly.

pop [pap] v. 급히 놓다; 펑 하는 소리가 나다; 잡다; n. 팝(뮤직); 펑 (하고 터지는 소리)
If you pop something somewhere, you put it there quickly.

crook [kruk] n. 사기꾼; v. (손가락이나 팔을) 구부리다
A crook is a dishonest person or a criminal.

bust [bʌst] v. (경찰이) 불시 단속을 벌이다; 급습하다; 부수다; 고장 내다; n. 흉상, 반신상
If someone is busted, the police arrest them.

bulb [bʌlb] n. (양파 등의) 구근(球根); 전구
A bulb is a root shaped like an onion that grows into a flower or plant.

Check Your Reading Speed
1분에 몇 단어를 읽는지 리딩 속도를 측정해보세요.

$$\frac{296 \text{ words}}{\text{reading time (} \quad \text{) sec}} \times 60 = (\quad) \text{ WPM}$$

Build Your Vocabulary

* **junk** [dʒʌŋk] n. 쓸모없는 물건, 폐물, 쓰레기; v. 폐물로 처분하다
  Junk is old and used goods that have little value and that you do not want any more.

* **release** [rilíːs] v. 공개하다, 발표하다; 놓아 주다; (감정을) 발산하다; n. 석방; 발표, 공개
  When an entertainer or company releases a new CD, video, or film, it becomes available so that people can buy it or see it.

  knock-off [nak-ɔ́ːf] n. (유명 메이커 의류 등의) 모조품, 가짜; (일 등의) 중지
  A knock-off is a cheap copy of a well-known product.

  bootleg [búːtlèg] a. (제작·판매가) 불법의, 해적판의
  Bootleg is used to describe something that is made secretly and sold illegally.

  melt [melt] v. 녹다; (감정 등이) 누그러지다; n. 용해
  When a solid substance melts or when you melt it, it changes to a liquid, usually because it has been heated.

  recognize [rékəgnàiz] v. 알아보다; 인식하다; 공인하다
  If you recognize someone or something, you know who that person is or what that thing is.

  moldy [móuldi] a. 곰팡이가 핀; 케케묵은
  Something that is moldy is covered with mold.

  flick [flik] v. 튀기다, 털다; 잽싸게 움직이다; n. 재빨리 움직임
  If something flicks in a particular direction, or if someone flicks it, it moves with a short, sudden movement.

  toothpick [túːθpik] n. 이쑤시개
  A toothpick is a small stick which you use to remove food from between your teeth.

  exact [igzǽkt] a. 정확한, 정밀한; 꼼꼼한, 빈틈없는
  Exact means correct in every detail.

pit [pit] n. (크고 깊은) 구덩이; v. 자국을 남기다, 구멍을 남기다
A pit is a large hole that is dug in the ground.

squirm [skwəːrm] v. (몸을) 꿈틀대다; 몹시 창피해 하다
If you squirm, you move your body from side to side, usually because you are nervous or uncomfortable.

motion [móuʃən] v. (손·머리로) 몸짓을 해 보이다; n. 운동, 움직임; 동작, 몸짓
If you motion to someone, you move your hand or head as a way of telling them to do something or telling them where to go.

dangle [dǽŋgl] v. (무엇을 들고) 달랑거리다; 매달리다
If something dangles from somewhere or if you dangle it somewhere, it hangs or swings loosely.

emerge [imə́ːrdʒ] v. 나오다, 모습을 드러내다; (어려움 등을) 헤쳐 나오다
To emerge means to come out from an enclosed or dark space such as a room or a vehicle, or from a position where you could not be seen.

show off idiom ~을 자랑하다; 돋보이게 하다
To show off someone or something means to try to make people pay attention to them because you are proud of them.

pregnant [prégnənt] a. 임신한
If a woman or female animal is pregnant, she has a baby or babies developing in her body.

belly [béli] n. 배, 복부
The belly of a person or animal is their stomach or abdomen.

dough [dou] n. 돈; 밀가루 반죽
You can refer to money as dough.

drop [drap] n. 비밀 장물 은닉 장소; 방울; 소량, 조금; v. 떨어뜨리다; 약해지다; 낮추다
A drop is the act of leaving or delivering something in a place that has been agreed, especially something secret or illegal.

spot [spat] n. (특정한) 곳; (작은) 점; v. 발견하다, 찾다, 알아채다
You can refer to a particular place as a spot.

underground [ʌndərgráund] ad. 지하에; a. 지하의
Something that is underground is below the surface of the ground.

watch it idiom 조심해!; 그러지 마!, 그러면 안 돼!
You can say 'watch it' to warn someone to be careful.

^{복습} **friendly** [fréndli] a. 상냥한, 다정한; (행동이) 친절한; 우호적인

If someone is friendly, they behave in a pleasant, kind way, and like to be with other people.

CHAPTERS 25 & 26

1. **How did Doug make the animals go savage?**
    A. He sold the night howlers simply as flowers.
    B. He planted night howlers throughout Zootopia.
    C. He put night howler serum into pellets and shot them.
    D. He poisoned their drinking water with night howlers.

2. **How did Judy want to get the evidence back to ZPD?**
    A. She wanted to only bring what she and Nick could carry.
    B. She wanted to bring the whole subway car on the tracks.
    C. She wanted Nick to carry the evidence while she distracted Doug.
    D. She wanted to destroy the train to stop the spread of night howlers.

3. **How did Bellwether know where Judy and Nick would be?**
   A. The ZPD had called Bellwether for help.
   B. Judy had called Bellwether for help in the subway.
   C. Bellwether had been behind everything from the beginning.
   D. Bellwether had heard the subway car explosion and wanted to help.

4. **Why was Bellwether creating fear against predators?**
   A. She worried about the safety of prey.
   B. She never truly believed in the idea of Zootopia.
   C. She thought that predators were already really savage.
   D. She wanted to create fear so that she could stay in power.

5. **Why did Nick NOT go savage after Bellwether shot him?**
   A. Nick was immune to the effects of night howlers.
   B. Bellwether had missed Nick when she shot.
   C. Bellwether had shot Nick with blueberries.
   D. Nick cared about Judy too much to attack her.

Check Your Reading Speed
1분에 몇 단어를 읽는지 리딩 속도를 측정해보세요.

$$\frac{650 \text{ words}}{\text{reading time (}\quad\text{) sec}} \times 60 = (\qquad) \text{ WPM}$$

Build Your Vocabulary

- **instruction** [instrʌ́kʃən] n. 설명; 지시
  An instruction is something that someone tells you to do.

- **drop** [drap] n. 비밀 장물 은닉 장소; 방울; 소량, 조금; v. 떨어뜨리다; 약해지다; 낮추다
  A drop is the act of leaving or delivering something in a place that has been agreed, especially something secret or illegal.

- **abandon** [əbǽndən] v. 버리고 떠나다; 버리다; 그만두다 (abandoned a. 버려진, 유기된)
  An abandoned place or building is no longer used or occupied.

- **peek** [piːk] v. (재빨리) 훔쳐보다; 살짝 보이다; n. 엿보기
  If you peek at something or someone, you have a quick look at them, often secretly.

- **whisper** [hwíspər] v. 속삭이다, 소곤거리다; 은밀히 말하다; n. 속삭임, 소곤거리는 소리
  When you whisper, you say something very quietly, using your breath rather than your throat, so that only one person can hear you.

- **interior** [intíəriər] n. 내부; a. 내부의
  The interior of something is the inside part of it.

- **transform** [trænsfɔ́ːrm] v. 변형시키다; 완전히 바꿔 놓다
  To transform something into something else means to change or convert it into that thing.

- **greenhouse** [gríːnhàus] n. 온실
  A greenhouse is a glass building in which you grow plants that need to be protected from bad weather.

- **row** [rou] n. 열, 줄; 노 젓기; v. 노를 젓다
  A row of things or people is a number of them arranged in a line.

corner [kɔ́:rnər] v. (특정 상품의) 시장을 장악하다; (구석에) 가두다; (궁지에) 몰아넣다;
n. 모퉁이; 구석
If a company or place corners an area of trade, they gain control over it so that no one else can have any success in that area.

click [klik] n. 찰칵 (하는 소리); (마우스를) 클릭함; v. 딸깍 하는 소리를 내다; (마우스를) 클릭하다
A click is a short, sharp sound.

lab [læb] n. (= laboratory) 실험실, 연구실 (lab coat n. 실험실 가운)
A lab is the same as a laboratory, which is a building or a room where scientific experiments, analyses, and research are carried out.

flowering [fláuəriŋ] a. 꽃이 있는, 꽃이 피는; n. 개화기; 전성기
Flowering shrubs, trees, or plants are those which produce noticeable flowers.

harvest [há:rvist] v. 수확하다, 거둬들이다; 채취하다; n. 수확; 수확물
When you harvest a crop, you gather it in.

pollen [pálən] n. 꽃가루, 화분
Pollen is a fine powder produced by flowers. It fertilizes other flowers of the same species so that they produce seeds.

pellet [pélit] n. 알갱이; 아주 작은 총알
A pellet is a small ball of paper, mud, lead, or other material.

serum [síərəm] n. 혈청
A serum is a liquid that is injected into someone's blood to protect them against a poison or disease.

disbelief [dìsbilí:f] n. 믿기지 않음, 불신감
Disbelief is not believing that something is true or real.

mark [ma:rk] n. 표적, 목표물; 자국; 표시; v. 표시하다; 자국을 내다
A mark means a target.

square [skwɛər] n. (시가지의) 한 구획, 가구; 광장; 정사각형; 제곱; a. 정사각형 모양의; 직각의
In a town or city, a square is a flat open place, often in the shape of a square.

load [loud] v. (무기에 탄환 등을) 장전하다; (짐·사람 등을) 싣다; 가득 안겨 주다; n. (많은 양의) 짐
When someone loads a weapon such as a gun, they put a bullet or missile in it so that it is ready to use.

cock [kak] v. (총의) 공이치기를 당기다; 몸을 뒤로 젖히다; n. 수탉
If you cock a gun, you raise the hammer on the gun so that it is ready to fire.

tiny [táini] a. 아주 작은
Something or someone that is tiny is extremely small.

contain [kəntéin] v. ~이 들어 있다: (감정을) 억누르다
If writing, speech, or film contains particular information, ideas, or images, it includes them.

buzz [bʌz] v. 전화를 걸다: 윙윙거리다: 부산스럽다, 활기가 넘치다: n. 윙윙거리는 소리
If you buzz someone, you give them a call.

bam [bæm] int. 퍽, 쿵 (하고 부딪치는 소리)
Bam is a sudden very loud noise, as that produced when two objects strike against each other with force.

bang [bæŋ] v. 쾅 하고 치다: 쾅 하고 닫다: 쿵 하고 찧다: n. 쾅 (하는 소리)
If you bang on something or if you bang it, you hit it hard, making a loud noise.

let in idiom ~을 들어오게 하다
If you let someone or something in, you allow them to enter a room or a building.

wham [hwæm] int. 쾅, 쿵 (세게 부딪치는 소리)
Wham is used to suggest the sound of a sudden hit.

knock [nak] v. 치다, 부딪치다: (문 등을) 두드리다: n. 문 두드리는 소리: 부딪침
(knock into idiom ~에 부딪치다)
If you knock something, you touch or hit it roughly, especially so that it falls or moves.

lock [lak] v. (자물쇠로) 잠그다: 고정시키다: n. 잠금장치
When you lock something such as a door, drawer, or case, you fasten it, usually with a key, so that other people cannot open it.

shut out idiom ~을 못 들어가게 하다
If you shut someone or something out, you stop them from entering or getting back inside a house or other building.

surround [səráund] v. 둘러싸다, 에워싸다: 포위하다
If a person or thing is surrounded by something, that thing is situated all around them.

pound [paund] v. (여러 차례) 치다, 두드리다: 쿵쾅거리며 걷다
If you pound something or pound on it, you hit it with great force, usually loudly and repeatedly.

evidence [évədəns] n. 증거, 흔적; v. 증언하다; 증거가 되다
Evidence is anything that you see, experience, read, or are told that causes you to believe that something is true or has really happened.

conductor [kəndʌ́ktər] n. (버스나 기차의) 안내원; 지휘자
On a train, a conductor is a person whose job is to travel on the train in order to help passengers and check tickets.

rust [rʌst] n. 녹; v. 녹슬다, 부식하다 (rust bucket n. 녹슨 차)
A rust bucket refers to something that is run-down or old, especially a very badly rusted car.

fire [faiər] v. (엔진이) 점화되다; 해고하다; 사격하다; 발사하다; n. 화재, 불
When the engine of a motor vehicle fires, an electrical spark is produced which causes the fuel to burn and the engine to work.

defeat [difíːt] n. 패배; v. 좌절시키다; 패배시키다; 물리치다; 이해가 안 되다
Defeat is the experience of being beaten in a battle, game, or contest, or of failing to achieve what you wanted to.

track [træk] n. (기차) 선로; 길; 자국; v. 추적하다; (자취 등을 따라) 뒤쫓다; 발자국을 남기다
Railway tracks are the rails that a train travels along.

accomplish [əkámpliʃ] v. 완수하다, 성취하다, 해내다
If you accomplish something, you succeed in doing it.

premature [prìːməʃúər] a. 너무 이른, 시기상조의; 조급한
You can say that something is premature when it happens too early and is therefore inappropriate.

toot [tuːt] n. 빵, 삑 (하는 경적·호루라기 소리); v. (빵 하고 자동차) 경적을 울리다
A toot is a short, sharp sound made by a horn, trumpet, or similar instrument.

gesture [dʒésʧər] v. (손·머리 등으로) 가리키다; 몸짓을 하다; n. 몸짓; (감정·의도의) 표시
If you gesture, you use movements of your hands or head in order to tell someone something or draw their attention to something.

whistle [hwisl] n. (기차·배 등의) 기적, 경적; 휘파람 (소리); v. 휘파람을 불다; 기적을 울리다
A whistle is an instrument used to produce a shrill, high-pitched sound, especially for giving a signal.

burst [bəːrst] v. (burst-burst) 불쑥 움직이다; 터지다, 파열하다; n. (갑자기) 한바탕 ~을 함; 파열
To burst into or out of a place means to enter or leave it suddenly with a lot of energy or force.

windshield [wíndʃiːld] n. (자동차 등의) 앞 유리
The windshield of a car or other vehicle is the glass window at the front through which the driver looks.

headbutt [hédbʌt] v. (머리로) 들이받다
If someone headbutts you, they hit you with the top of their head.

hail [heil] n. 우박; ~의 빗발; v. 우박이 쏟아지다; 신호를 보내다
Hail consists of small balls of ice that fall like rain from the sky.

joke [dʒouk] v. 농담하다, 재미있는 이야기를 하다; 농담 삼아 말하다; n. 우스개, 농담; 웃음거리
If you joke, you tell someone something that is not true in order to amuse yourself.

boom [buːm] n. 쾅 (하는 소리); v. 쾅 하는 소리를 내다; 굵은 목소리로 말하다
Boom can refer to a loud, deep, resonant sound.

bust [bʌst] v. 부수다; 고장 내다; (경찰이) 불시 단속을 벌이다, 급습하다; n. 흉상, 반신상
If you bust something, you break it or damage it so badly that it cannot be used.

grab [græb] v. (와락·단단히) 붙잡다; 급히 ~하다; n. 와락 잡아채려고 함
If you grab something, you take it or pick it up suddenly and roughly.

horn [hoːrn] n. (양·소 등의) 뿔; (차량의) 경적
The horns of an animal such as a cow or deer are the hard pointed things that grow from its head.

chug [tʃʌg] v. 칙칙폭폭 소리를 내며 나아가다; n. (엔진이 내는) 칙칙 (하는 소리)
When a vehicle chugs somewhere, it goes there slowly, noisily and with difficulty.

split second [split sékənd] n. 아주 짧은 순간; 눈 깜짝할 사이
A split second is an extremely short period of time.

crash [kræʃ] v. 충돌하다, 들이받다; 부딪치다; 굉음을 내다; n. (자동차·항공기) 사고; 요란한 소리
If a moving vehicle crashes or if the driver crashes it, it hits something and is damaged or destroyed.

switch [swiʧ] n. 스위치; 전환; v. 전환하다, 바꾸다
A switch is a place on a railway track where the rails can be moved to allow a train to change from one track to another.

lever [lévər] n. (기계·차량 조작용) 레버; 지레; 수단; v. 지렛대로 움직이다
A lever is a handle or bar that is attached to a piece of machinery and which you push or pull in order to operate the machinery.

derail [di:réil] v. (기차가) 탈선하다; (계획 등을) 틀어지게 하다
If a train is derailed or if it derails, it comes off the track on which it is running.

dive [daiv] v. (dove–dived) 급히 움직이다; (물 속으로) 뛰어들다; 급강하하다;
n. (물 속으로) 뛰어들기
If you dive in a particular direction or into a particular place, you jump or move
there quickly.

platform [plǽtfɔ:rm] n. (기차역의) 플랫폼; 연단, 강단; (장비 등을 올려놓는) 대(臺)
A platform in a railway station is the area beside the rails where you wait for or get
off a train.

explode [iksplóud] v. 터지다, 폭발하다; (갑자기 강한 감정을) 터뜨리다
If an object such as a bomb explodes or if someone or something explodes it, it
bursts loudly and with great force, often causing damage or injury.

include [inklú:d] v. 포함하다; ~을 (~에) 포함시키다
If one thing includes another thing, it has the other thing as one of its parts.

burn to a crisp idiom 새까맣게 태우다, 바싹 태우다
If you burn something to a crisp, you burn it completely, leaving only a charred
remnant.

Check Your Reading Speed

1분에 몇 단어를 읽는지 리딩 속도를 측정해보세요.

$$\frac{942 \text{ words}}{\text{reading time (\quad) sec}} \times 60 = (\qquad) \text{ WPM}$$

Build Your Vocabulary

race [reis] v. 쏜살같이 가다; 경주하다; 정신없이 돌아가다; n. 경주; 경쟁; 인종, 종족
If you race somewhere, you go there as quickly as possible.

statue [stǽtʃuː] n. 조각상
A statue is a large sculpture of a person or an animal, made of stone or metal.

exhibit [igzíbit] n. 전시품; v. 전시하다; 보이다, 드러내다
An exhibit is a painting, sculpture, or object of interest that is displayed to the public in a museum or art gallery.

evolution [èvəlúːʃən] n. (점진적인) 발전; 진화
Evolution is a process of gradual development in a particular situation or thing over a period of time.

cop [kap] n. 경찰관
A cop is a policeman or policewoman.

mayor [méiər] n. (시·군 등의) 시장
The mayor of a town or city is the person who has been elected to represent it for a fixed period of time or, in some places, to run its government.

dart [daːrt] v. (화살 등을) 쏘다; 쏜살같이 움직이다; 흘깃 쳐다보다; n. (작은) 화살; 쏜살같이 달림
To dart means to shoot an animal with a dart, typically in order to administer a drug.

predator [prédətər] n. 포식자, 포식 동물; 약탈자
A predator is an animal that kills and eats other animals.

serum [síərəm] n. 혈청
A serum is a liquid that is injected into someone's blood to protect them against a poison or disease.

- **applaud** [əplɔ́ːd] v. 박수를 치다; 갈채를 보내다
When a group of people applaud, they clap their hands in order to show approval, for example when they have enjoyed a play or concert.

- **suspicious** [səspíʃəs] a. 의혹을 갖는, 수상쩍어 하는; 의심스러운
If you are suspicious of someone or something, you believe that they are probably involved in a crime or some dishonest activity.

- **block** [blak] v. 막다, 차단하다; 방해하다; n. 구역, 블록; 사각형 덩어리
If you block someone's way, you prevent them from going somewhere or entering a place by standing in front of them.

- **all of a sudden** idiom 갑자기
If something happens all of a sudden, it happens quickly and unexpectedly.

- **crystal clear** [krístl klíər] a. 명명백백한, 아주 분명한; 수정같이 맑은
If you say that a message or statement is crystal clear, you are emphasizing that it is very easy to understand.

- **signal** [sígnəl] v. (동작·소리로) 신호를 보내다; 암시하다; n. 신호; 징조
If you signal to someone, you make a gesture or sound in order to send them a particular message.

- **dash** [dæʃ] v. (급히) 서둘러 가다; 내동댕이치다; n. 돌진, 질주; 단거리 경주
If you dash somewhere, you run or go there quickly and suddenly.

- **corridor** [kɔ́ːridər] n. 복도; 통로
A corridor is a long passage in a building or train, with doors and rooms on one or both sides.

- **glance** [glæns] v. 흘깃 보다; 대충 훑어보다; n. 흘깃 봄
If you glance at something or someone, you look at them very quickly and then look away again immediately.

- **tusk** [tʌsk] n. (코끼리의) 상아; (삽 등의) 뾰족한 끝
The tusks of an elephant, wild boar, or walrus are its two very long, curved, pointed teeth.

- **slash** [slæʃ] v. 긋다, 베다; 대폭 줄이다; n. (칼 등으로) 긋기
If you slash something, you make a long, deep cut in it.

- **knock** [nak] v. 치다, 부딪치다; (문 등을) 두드리다; n. 문 두드리는 소리; 부딪침
To knock someone into a particular position or condition means to hit them very hard so that they fall over or become unconscious.

rush [rʌʃ] v. 급(속)히 움직이다; 서두르다; 재촉하다; n. 혼잡, 분주함
If you rush somewhere, you go there quickly.

bleed [bliːd] v. 피를 흘리다. 출혈하다
When you bleed, you lose blood from your body as a result of injury or illness.

pillar [pílər] n. (둥근) 기둥; 기둥 모양의 것; 대들보
A pillar is a tall solid structure, which is usually used to support part of a building.

whisper [hwíspər] v. 속삭이다, 소곤거리다; 은밀히 말하다; n. 속삭임, 소곤거리는 소리
When you whisper, you say something very quietly, using your breath rather than your throat, so that only one person can hear you.

surrender [səréndər] v. 항복하다, 투항하다; (권리 등을) 포기하다; n. 항복, 굴복
If you surrender, you stop fighting or resisting someone and agree that you have been beaten.

underestimate [ʌ̀ndəréstəmeit] v. 과소평가하다; (비용·규모 등을) 너무 적게 잡다; n. 과소평가
If you underestimate someone, you do not realize what they are capable of doing.

underappreciated [ʌ̀ndərəpríːʃieitid] a. 인정을 덜 받는, 정당하게 평가되지 못하는
If someone or something is underappreciated, they are not valued sufficiently highly.

prey [prei] n. 먹이, 사냥감; 희생자, 피해자
A creature's prey are the creatures that it hunts and eats in order to live.

outnumber [autnʌ́mbər] v. ~보다 수가 많다, 수적으로 우세하다
If one group of people or things outnumbers another, the first group has more people or things in it than the second group.

population [pàpjuléiʃən] n. 인구, (모든) 주민
The population of a country or area is all the people who live in it.

unite [juːnáit] v. 연합하다; 통합시키다, 결속시키다
If a group of people or things unite or if something unites them, they join together and act as a group.

unstoppable [ʌnstápəbl] a. 막을 수 없는
Something that is unstoppable cannot be prevented from continuing or developing.

spot [spat] v. 발견하다, 찾다, 알아채다; n. (작은) 점; (특정한) 곳
If you spot something or someone, you notice them.

gesture [dʒéstʃər] v. (손·머리 등으로) 가리키다; 몸짓을 하다; n. 몸짓; (감정·의도의) 표시
If you gesture, you use movements of your hands or head in order to tell someone something or draw their attention to something.

pounce [pauns] v. (공격하거나 잡으려고 확) 덮치다, 덤비다
If someone pounces on you, they come up toward you suddenly and take hold of you.

mummify [mʌ́məfài] v. (시체를) 미라로 만들다
If a dead body is mummified, it is preserved, for example by rubbing it with special oils and wrapping it in cloth.

make a run for it idiom 필사적으로 도망치다, (위험을) 서둘러 피하다
If you make a run for it or if you run for it, you run away in order to escape from someone or something.

whack [wæk] n. 퍽, 철썩 (하고 세게 치는 소리); 강타, 후려치기; v. 세게 치다, 후려치다
A whack is the act of hitting someone or something with a lot of force, or the sound that it makes.

tackle [tækl] v. 달려들다; (힘든 문제·상황과) 씨름하다; n. 태클
If you tackle someone, you attack them and fight them.

grip [grip] n. 꽉 붙잡음, 움켜쥠; 통제; v. 꽉 잡다, 움켜쥐다; (마음·시선을) 끌다
A grip is a firm, strong hold on something.

sunken [sʌ́ŋkən] a. (주변 지역보다) 낮은; 침몰한; (눈·볼이) 움푹 들어간
Sunken gardens, roads, or other features are below the level of their surrounding area.

edge [edʒ] n. 끝, 가장자리; 우위; v. 조금씩 움직이다; 테두리를 두르다
The edge of something is the place or line where it stops, or the part of it that is furthest from the middle.

yell [jel] v. 고함치다, 소리 지르다; n. 고함, 외침
If you yell, you shout loudly, usually because you are excited, angry, or in pain.

crouch [krautʃ] v. (몸을) 쭈그리다, 쭈그리고 앉다; n. 쭈그리고 앉기
If you are crouching, your legs are bent under you so that you are close to the ground and leaning forward slightly.

dial [dáiəl] v. 다이얼을 돌리다, 전화를 걸다; n. (시계·계기 등의) 문자반
If you dial or if you dial a number, you turn the dial or press the buttons on a telephone in order to phone someone.

officer [ɔ́ːfisər] n. 순경; 경찰관; 장교
Members of the police force can be referred to as officers.

biological [bàiəládʒikəl] a. 생물체의; 생물학의 (biologically ad. 생물학적으로)
Biological is used to describe processes and states that occur in the bodies and cells of living things.

predispose [priːdispóuz] v. ~하게 만들다, ~하는 성향을 갖게 하다; 취약하게 하다
If something predisposes you to think or behave in a particular way, it makes it likely that you will think or behave in that way.

stalk [stɔːk] v. 몰래 접근하다; (화가 난 듯이) 성큼성큼 걷다; n. (식물의) 줄기
If you stalk a person or a wild animal, you follow them quietly in order to kill them, catch them, or observe them carefully.

helpless [hélplis] a. 무력한, 속수무책인 (helplessly ad. 어찌해 볼 수도 없이)
If you are helpless, you do not have the strength or power to do anything useful or to control or protect yourself.

limp [limp] v. 다리를 절다, 절뚝거리다; n. 절뚝거림; a. 기운이 없는, 축 처진
If a person or animal limps, they walk with difficulty or in an uneven way because one of their legs or feet is hurt.

gosh [gaʃ] int. (놀람·기쁨을 나타내어) 어머!, 뭐라고!
Some people say 'Gosh' when they are surprised.

headline [hédlain] n. (신문 기사의) 표제; v. (기사에) 표제를 달다
A headline is the title of a newspaper story, printed in large letters at the top of the story, especially on the front page.

pleased [pliːzd] a. 기쁜, 기뻐하는, 만족해하는
If you are pleased, you are happy about something or satisfied with something.

growl [graul] v. 으르렁거리다; 으르렁거리듯 말하다; n. 으르렁거리는 소리
When a dog or other animal growls, it makes a low noise in its throat, usually because it is angry.

corner [kɔ́ːrnər] v. (구석에) 가두다, (궁지에) 몰아넣다; (특정 상품의) 시장을 장악하다; n. 모퉁이; 구석
If you corner a person or animal, you force them into a place they cannot escape from.

lunge [lʌndʒ] v. 달려들다, 돌진하다; n. 돌진
If you lunge in a particular direction, you move in that direction suddenly and clumsily.

confuse [kənfjúːz] v. (사람을) 혼란시키다; 혼동하다 (confused a. 혼란스러워하는)
If you are confused, you do not know exactly what is happening or what to do.

milk [milk] v. (최대한) 뽑아내다; 우유를 짜다; n. 우유
If you say that someone milks something, you mean that they get as much benefit or profit as they can from it, without caring about the effects this has on other people.

lay out idiom (계획·주장 등을 잘 정리하여) 제시하다; (보기 좋게) ~을 배치하다
If you lay something out, you present or explain it clearly and carefully.

figure out idiom ~을 이해하다, 알아내다; 계산하다, 산출하다
If you figure out someone or something, you come to understand them by thinking carefully.

weapon [wépən] n. 무기, 흉기
A weapon is an object such as a gun, a knife, or a missile, which is used to kill or hurt people in a fight or a war.

lick [lik] v. 핥다; 핥아먹다; n. 한 번 핥기; 핥아먹기
When people or animals lick something, they move their tongue across its surface.

chamber [ʧéimbər] n. (기계의) ~실(室); 회의실; (지하의) 공간
A chamber is a closed space in a machine, plant, or body.

frame [freim] v. 죄를 뒤집어씌우다; 틀에 넣다, 테를 두르다; n. (가구·건물 등의) 뼈대; 틀, 액자
If someone frames an innocent person, they make other people think that that person is guilty of a crime, by lying or inventing evidence.

press [pres] v. 누르다; (무엇에) 바짝 대다; 꾹 밀어 넣다; n. 언론; 인쇄
If you press a button or switch, you push it with your finger in order to make a machine or device work.

hustle [hʌsl] n. 사기; 법석, 혼잡; v. (사람을 거칠게) 떠밀다; (불법적으로) 팔다
A hustle is a dishonest way of making money.

sweetheart [swíːthàːrt] n. (애정을 담아 부르는 호칭으로) 자기, 애야
You call someone sweetheart if you are very fond of them.

CHAPTERS 27 & 28

1. **How did Lionheart feel about imprisoning the animals?**
   A. He felt terrible and decided to stay in jail.
   B. He felt that he did the wrong thing for the right reason.
   C. He felt that he could do anything he wanted as the mayor.
   D. He felt that he was just trying to protect the savage animals.

2. **What happened to the victims of the night howler darts after Bellwether went to jail?**
   A. An antivenom was developed to help the victims.
   B. The victims were still savage and locked away.
   C. The victims were moved for away from Zootopia.
   D. The victims naturally recovered over time.

3. What happened to Nick after the case was solved?

A. Nick was arrested for tax evasion.

B. Nick became the new assistant mayor of Zootopia.

C. Nick joined the ZPD and became Judy's partner.

D. Nick went back to selling pawpsicles on the street.

4. What were Judy and Nick assigned to on the ZPD?

A. Parking duty

B. Missing animals cases

C. Parade duty

D. Traffic duty

5. How had Judy and Nick's attitudes changed at the end?

A. They were still angry at each other.

B. They were still suspicious of each other.

C. They were both bored being police officers.

D. They were comfortable enough to joke with each other.

Check Your Reading Speed

1분에 몇 단어를 읽는지 리딩 속도를 측정해보세요.

$$\frac{488 \text{ words}}{\text{reading time (\quad) sec}} \times 60 = (\qquad) \text{ WPM}$$

Build Your Vocabulary

channel [ʧǽnl] n. (텔레비전·라디오의) 채널;
v. (물·빛 등을) 보내다; (돈·감정·생각 등을) (~에) 쏟다
A channel is a television station.

footage [fútidʒ] n. (특정한 사건을 담은) 장면
Footage of a particular event is a film of it or the part of a film which shows this event.

jail [dʒeil] n. 교도소, 감옥; v. 수감하다
A jail is a place where criminals are kept in order to punish them, or where people waiting to be tried are kept.

mayor [méiər] n. (시·군 등의) 시장
The mayor of a town or city is the person who has been elected to represent it for a fixed period of time or, in some places, to run its government.

be behind bars idiom 교도소에 수감되다
If you say that someone is behind bars, you mean that they are in prison.

guilty [gílti] a. 유죄의; 죄책감이 드는, 가책을 느끼는
If someone is guilty of a crime or offence, they have committed that crime or offence.

mastermind [mǽstərmaind] v. 교묘히 지휘하다, 배후에서 조종하다;
n. (계획 등의) 지도자; (나쁜 짓의) 주모자
If you mastermind a difficult or complicated activity, you plan it in detail and then make sure that it happens successfully.

savage [sǽvidʒ] a. 야만적인, 흉포한; (비판 등이) 맹렬한; n. 포악한 사람; v. 흉포하게 공격하다
Someone or something that is savage is extremely cruel, violent, and uncontrolled.

* **plague** [pleig] v. (고통·문제로) 괴롭히다; 성가시게 하다; n. 전염병
If you are plagued by unpleasant things, they continually cause you a lot of trouble or suffering.

newscaster [njúːzkæstər] n. (라디오·텔레비전의) 뉴스 프로 진행자
A newscaster is a person who reads the news on the radio or on television.

prison [prizn] n. 교도소, 감옥
A prison is a building where criminals are kept as punishment or where people accused of a crime are kept before their trial.

* **predecessor** [prédəsèsər] n. 전임자
Your predecessor is the person who had your job before you.

* **plot** [plat] n. 음모; (소설·영화 등의) 구성; v. 음모하다; (소설·극 등의) 구성을 짜다
A plot is a secret plan by a group of people to do something that is illegal or wrong, usually against a person or a government.

imprison [imprízn] v. 투옥하다, 감금하다
If someone is imprisoned, they are locked up or kept somewhere, usually in prison as a punishment for a crime or for political opposition.

scenario [sinéəriòu] n. 예정된 계획; (사건의) 예상된 전개; (영화 등의) 각본
If you talk about a likely or possible scenario, you are talking about the way in which a situation may develop.

deadpan [dédpæn] ad. 무표정하게; a. 진지한 표정의, 무표정한; v. 무표정한 얼굴로 말하다
Deadpan humor is when you appear to be serious and are hiding the fact that you are joking or teasing someone.

howl [haul] v. (길게) 울다; (크고 시끄럽게) 울부짖다; n. (개·늑대 등의) 길게 짖는 소리
If an animal such as a wolf or a dog howls, it makes a long, loud, crying sound.

antivenom [æntivénəm] n. 해독제
Antivenom is an antitoxin active against the venom of a snake, spider, or other venomous animal or insect.

effective [iféktiv] a. 효과적인; 시행되는
Something that is effective works well and produces the results that were intended.

rehabilitate [riːhəbílətèit] v. (환자에게) 재활 치료를 하다; 회복시키다
To rehabilitate someone who has been ill or in prison means to help them to live a normal life again.

victim [víktim] n. (범죄·질병·사고 등의) 피해자
A victim is someone who has been hurt or killed.

grateful [gréitfəl] a. 고마워하는, 감사하는 (gratefully ad. 감사하여, 기뻐서)
If you are grateful for something that someone has given you or done for you, you have warm, friendly feelings toward them and wish to thank them.

lectern [léktərn] n. 연설대; 독서대
A lectern is a high sloping desk on which someone puts their notes when they are standing up and giving a lecture.

commencement [kəménsmənt] n. 학위 수여식, 졸업식; 시작, 개시
Commencement is a ceremony at a university, college, or high school at which students formally receive their degrees or diplomas.

address [ədrés] n. 연설; 주소; v. 연설하다; 말을 걸다; 주소를 쓰다
An address is a formal speech delivered to an audience.

graduate [grǽdʒuət] n. 졸업자; v. 졸업하다, 학위를 받다
In the United States, a graduate is a student who has successfully completed a course at a high school, college, or university.

get along idiom 사이좋게 지내다; 어울리다
If people get along, they like each other and are friendly to each other.

turn out idiom ~인 것으로 드러나다; 되어 가다; 나타나다
If things turn out, they are discovered or they prove to be the case finally and surprisingly.

complicated [kámpləkèitid] a. 복잡한, 이해하기 어려운
If you say that something is complicated, you mean it has so many parts or aspects that it is difficult to understand or deal with.

slogan [slóugən] n. 구호, 슬로건
A slogan is a short phrase that is easy to remember.

messy [mési] a. (상황이) 엉망인, 골치 아픈; 지저분한, 엉망인
If you describe a situation as messy, you are emphasizing that it is confused or complicated, and therefore unsatisfactory.

limitation [lìmətéiʃən] n. (능력 등의) 한계, 한정, 제한; 제약
If you talk about the limitations of someone or something, you mean that they can only do some things and not others, or cannot do something very well.

* **exceptional** [iksépʃənl] a. 이례적일 정도로 우수한, 특출한; 극히 예외적인
You use exceptional to describe someone or something that has a particular quality, usually a good quality, to an unusually high degree.

* **implore** [implɔ́ːr] v. 애원하다, 간청하다
If you implore someone to do something, you ask them to do it in a forceful, emotional way.

recognize [rékəgnàiz] v. 인식하다; 알아보다; 공인하다
If someone says that they recognize something, they acknowledge that it exists or that it is true.

pin [pin] v. (핀으로) 고정시키다; 꼼짝 못하게 하다; n. 핀
If you pin something on or to something, you attach it with a pin, a drawing pin, or a safety pin.

badge [bædʒ] n. (경찰 등의) 신분증; 표, 배지
A badge is a piece of metal or cloth which you wear to show that you belong to an organization or support a cause.

applause [əplɔ́ːz] n. 박수 (갈채)
Applause is the noise made by a group of people clapping their hands to show approval.

cadet [kədét] n. (경찰·군대의) 간부 후보생
A cadet is a young man or woman who is being trained in the armed services or the police.

chief [tʃiːf] n. (단체의) 최고위자; 추장, 족장; a. 주된; (계급·직급상) 최고위자인
The chief of an organization is the person who is in charge of it.

cop [kap] n. 경찰관
A cop is a policeman or policewoman.

recruit [rikrúːt] n. 신임 경찰; 신병; 새로운 구성원; v. 모집하다; (남을) 설득하다
A recruit is a person who has recently joined an organization or an army.

include [inklúːd] v. 포함하다; ~을 (~에) 포함시키다
If one thing includes another thing, it has the other thing as one of its parts.

line [lain] n. (상품의) 종류; 선, 줄; v. 줄을 세우다
A line is a particular type of product that a company makes or sells.

inspirational [inspəréiʃənl] a. 영감을 주는
Something that is inspirational provides you with a feeling of enthusiasm.

greet [gri:t] v. 인사하다; 환영하다; 반응을 보이다 (greeting card n. (생일 등의) 인사 카드)
A greeting card is a folded card with a picture on the front and greetings inside that you give or send to someone, for example on their birthday.

sarcastic [sɑːrkǽstik] a. 빈정대는, 비꼬는; 풍자적인 (sarcastically ad. 비꼬는 투로)
Someone who is sarcastic says or does the opposite of what they really mean in order to mock or insult someone.

assign [əsáin] v. (일·책임 등을) 맡기다; (사람을) 배치하다; ~의 탓으로 하다
(assignment n. 과제, 임무)
An assignment is a task or piece of work that you are given to do, especially as part of your job or studies.

parade [pəréid] n. 퍼레이드, 가두 행진; v. 가두 행진을 하다; (과시하듯) 걸어 다니다
A parade is a procession of people or vehicles moving through a public place in order to celebrate an important day or event.

dismiss [dismís] v. (사람을) 해산시키다; 묵살하다; (생각·느낌을) 떨쳐 버리다
If you are dismissed by someone in authority, they tell you that you can go away from them.

detail [ditéil] n. 특별 임무; 세부 사항; v. 상세히 알리다; (군인에게) 특별 임무를 부여하다
A detail is a particular job given to a group of soldiers or police officers.

Check Your Reading Speed

1분에 몇 단어를 읽는지 리딩 속도를 측정해보세요.

$$\frac{114 \text{ words}}{\text{reading time ( ) sec}} \times 60 = (\qquad) \text{ WPM}$$

Build Your Vocabulary

slam [slæm] v. 세게 밀다; 쾅 닫다; n. 쾅 하고 닫기; 탕 하는 소리
(slam on the brakes idiom 급브레이크를 밟다)
If you slam on the brakes of a vehicle, you operate them suddenly and with force.

lurch [ləːrʧ] v. (갑자기) 휘청하다; (공포·흥분으로) 떨리다; n. 휘청함; 요동침
To lurch means to make a sudden movement, especially forward, in an uncontrolled way.

accidental [æksədéntl] a. 우연한, 돌발적인 (accidentally ad. 우연히, 뜻하지 않게)
An accidental event happens by chance or as the result of an accident, and is not deliberately intended.

jam [dʒæm] v. 밀어 넣다; 움직이지 못하게 되다; n. 교통 체증; 혼잡; 잼
If you jam something somewhere, you push or put it there roughly.

sly [slai] a. 교활한, 음흉한; 다 알고 있다는 듯한
If you describe someone as sly, you disapprove of them because they keep their feelings or intentions hidden and are clever at deceiving people.

wipe [waip] v. (먼지·물기 등을) 닦다; 지우다; n. (행주·걸레를 써서) 닦기
If you wipe something, you rub its surface to remove dirt or liquid from it.

dumb [dʌm] a. 멍청한, 바보 같은; 말을 못 하는
If you call a person dumb, you mean that they are stupid or foolish.

trick out idiom ~을 치장하다 (tricked-out a. 치장한)
If you trick something out, you decorate it in a particular way.

blast [blæst] v. (음악이) 쾅쾅 울리다; 폭파하다; 후려치다; n. 폭발; 맹비판
If you blast something such as a car horn, or if it blasts, it makes a sudden, loud sound. If something blasts music, or music blasts, the music is very loud.

siren [sáiərən] n. (신호·경보) 사이렌
A siren is a warning device which makes a long, loud noise.

stomp [stamp] v. 짓밟다; 쿵쿵거리며 걷다, 발을 구르다
If you stomp on someone or something, you step down hard on them.

take off idiom (서둘러) 떠나다; 날아오르다
If you take off, you leave somewhere suddenly or in a hurry.

chase [ʧeis] v. 뒤쫓다, 추적하다; 추구하다; n. 추적, 추격; 추구함
If you chase someone, or chase after them, you run after them or follow them
quickly in order to catch or reach them.

catch air idiom 높이 점프하다
If someone or something catches air, they make a big jump high off the ground.

수고하셨습니다!

드디어 끝까지 다 읽으셨군요! 축하드립니다! 여러분은 이 책을 통해 총 19,578개의 단어를 읽으셨고, 1,000개 이상의 어휘와 표현들을 익히셨습니다. 이 책에 나온 어휘는 다른 원서를 읽을 때도 빈번히 만날 수 있는 필수 어휘들입니다. 이 책을 읽었던 경험은 비슷한 수준의 다른 원서들을 읽을 때 큰 도움이 될 것입니다.

이제 자신의 상황에 맞게 원서를 반복해서 읽거나, 오디오북을 들어 볼 수 있습니다. 혹은 비슷한 수준의 다른 원서를 찾아 읽는 것도 좋습니다. 일단 원서를 완독한 뒤에 어떻게 계속 영어 공부를 이어갈 수 있을지, 아래에 제시되는 도움말을 꼼꼼히 살펴보고 각자 상황에 맞게 적용해 보세요!

리딩(Reading)을 확실하게 다지고 싶다면? 반복해서 읽어 보세요!

리딩 실력을 탄탄하게 다지고 싶다면, 같은 원서를 2~3번 반복해서 읽을 것을 권합니다. 같은 책을 여러 번 읽으면 지루할 것 같지만, 꼭 그렇지도 않습니다. 반복해서 읽을 때 처음과 주안점을 다르게 두면, 전혀 다른 느낌으로 재미있게 읽을 수 있습니다.

처음 원서를 읽을 때는 생소한 단어들과 스토리로 인해 읽으면서 곧바로 이해하기가 매우 힘들 수 있습니다. 전체 맥락을 잡고 읽어도 약간 버거운 느낌이지요. 하지만 반복해서 읽기 시작하면 달라집니다. 일단 내용을 파악한 상황이기 때문에 문장 구조나 어휘의 활용에 더 집중하게 되고, 조금 더 깊이 있게 읽을 수 있습니다. 좋은 표현과 문장을 수집하고 메모할 만한 여유도 생기게 되지요. 어휘도 많이 익숙해졌기 때문에 리딩 속도에도 탄력이 붙습니다. 처음 읽을 때는 '내용'에서 재미를 느꼈다면, 반복해서 읽을 때에는 '영어'에서 재미를 느끼게 되는 것입니다. 따라서 리닝 실력을 더욱 확고하게 다지고자 한다면, 같은 책을 2~3회 정도 반복해서 읽을 것을 권해 드립니다.

리스닝(Listening) 실력을 늘리고 싶다면? 귀를 통해서 읽어 보세요!

많은 영어 학습자들이 '리스닝이 안 돼서 문제'라고 한탄합니다. 그리고 리스닝 실력을 늘리는 방법으로 무슨 뜻인지 몰라도 반복해서 듣는 '무작정 듣기'를 선택합니다. 하지만 뜻도 모르면서 무작정 듣는 일에는 엄청난 인내력이 필요합니다. 그래서 대부분 며칠 시도하다가 포기해 버리고 말지요.

따라서 모르는 내용을 무작정 듣는 것보다는 어느 정도 알고 있는 내용을 반복해서 듣는 것이 더 효과적인 듣기 방법입니다. 그리고 이런 방식의 듣기에 활용할 수 있는 가장 좋은 교재가 오디오북입니다.

리스닝 실력을 향상하고 싶다면, 이 책에서 제공하는 오디오북을 이용해서 듣는 연습을 해 보세요. 활용법은 간단합니다. 일단 책을 한 번 완독했다면, 오디오북을 통해 다시 들어 보는 것입니다. 휴대 기기에 넣어 시간이 날 때 틈틈이 듣는 것도 좋고, 책상에 앉아 눈으로는 텍스트를 보며 귀로 읽는 것도 좋습니다. 이미 읽었던 내용이라 이해하기가 훨씬 수월하고, 애매했던 발음들도 자연스럽게 교정할 수 있습니다. 또 성우의 목소리 연기를 듣다 보면 내용이 더욱 생동감 있게 다가와 이해도가 높아지는 효과도 거둘 수 있습니다.

반대로 듣기에 자신 있는 사람이라면, 책을 읽기 전에 처음부터 오디오북을 먼저 듣는 것도 좋은 방법입니다. 귀를 통해 책을 쭉 읽어 보고, 이후에 다시 눈으로 책을 읽으면서 잘 들리지 않았던 부분을 보충하는 것이지요.

중요한 것은 내용을 따라가면서, 내용에 푹 빠져서 반복해 들어야 한다는 것입니다. 이렇게 연습을 반복해서 눈으로 읽지 않은 책이라도 '귀를 통해' 읽을 수 있을 정도가 되면, 리스닝으로 고생하는 일은 거의 없을 것입니다.

이 책은 미국 현지에서 정식으로 판매되고 있는 오디오북을 기본으로 제공하고 있습니다. 오디오북은 롱테일북스 홈페이지(www.longtailbooks.co.kr)에서도 다운로드 받을 수 있습니다. 오디오북에 이상이 있을 경우 team@ltinc.net으로 메일을 주시면 안내를 받으실 수 있습니다.

스피킹(Speaking)이 고민이라면? 소리 내어 읽어 보세요!

스피킹 역시 많은 학습자들이 고민하는 부분입니다. 스피킹이 고민이라면, 원서를 큰 소리로 읽는 낭독 훈련(voice reading)을 해 보세요!
'소리 내어 읽는 것이 말하기에 정말로 도움이 될까?'라고 의아한 생각이 들 수도 있습니다. 하지만 인간의 두뇌 입장에서 봤을 때, 성대 구조를 활용해서 '발화'한다는 점에서는 소리 내어 읽기와 말하기는 큰 차이가 없다고 합니다. 소리 내어 읽는 것은 '타인의 생각'을 전달하고, 직접 말하는 것은 '자신의 생각'을 전달한다는 차이가 있을 뿐, 머릿속에서 문장을 처리하고 조음기관(혀와 성대 등)을 움직여 의미를 만든다는 점에서 같은 과정인 것이지요. 따라서 소리 내어 읽는 연습을 꾸준히 하는 것은 스피킹 연습에 큰 도움이 됩니다.
소리 내어 읽기를 하는 방법은 간단합니다. 일단 오디오북을 들으면서 성우의 목소리를 최대한 따라 하며 같이 읽어 보세요. 발음뿐 아니라, 억양, 어조, 느낌까지 완벽히 따라 한다고 생각하면서 소리 내어 읽습니다. 따라 읽는 것이 조금 익숙해지면, 옆의 누군가에게 이 책을 읽어 준다는 생각으로 소리 내어 계속 읽어 나갑니다. 한 번 눈과 귀로 읽었던 책이기 때문에 보다 수월하게 진행할 수 있고, 자연스럽게 어휘와 표현을 복습하는 효과도 거두게 됩니다. 또 이렇게 소리 내어 읽은 것을 녹음해서 들어 보면 스스로에게도 좋은 피드백이 됩니다.

라이팅(Writing)까지 욕심이 난다면? 요약하는 연습을 해 보세요!

원서를 라이팅 연습에 직접적으로 활용하는 데에는 한계가 있지만, 적절히 활용하면 원서도 유용한 라이팅 자료가 될 수 있습니다.
특히 책을 읽고 그 내용을 요약하는 연습은 큰 도움이 됩니다. 요약 훈련의 방식도 간단합니다. 원서를 읽고 그날 읽은 분량만큼 혹은 책을 다 읽고 전체 내용을 기반으로, 책 내용을 한번 요약하고 나의 느낌을 영어로 적어 보는 것입니다.
이때 그 책에 나왔던 단어와 표현을 최대한 활용하여 요약하는 것이 중요합니다. 영어 표현력은 결국 얼마나 다양한 어휘로 많은 표현을 해 보았느냐가 좌우하게 됩니다. 이런 면에서 내가 읽은 책을, 그 책에 나온 문장과 어휘로 다시 표현해 보는 것은 매우 효율적인 방법입니다. 책에 나온 어휘와 표현을 단순히 읽고 무슨 말인지 아는 정도가 아니라, 실제로 직접 활용해서 쓸 수 있을 만큼 확실하게 익히게 되는 것이지요. 여기에 첨삭까지 받을 수 있는 방법이 있다면 금상첨화입니다.

이러한 '표현하기' 연습은 스피킹 훈련에도 그대로 적용될 수 있습니다. 책을 읽고 그 내용을 3분 안에 다른 사람에게 영어로 말하는 연습을 해 보세요. 순발력과 표현력을 기르는 좋은 훈련이 될 것입니다.

'스피드 리딩 카페'에서 함께 원서를 읽어 보세요!

원서 읽기를 활용한 영어 공부에 관심이 있으시다면, 국내 최대 영어원서 읽기 동호회 스피드 리딩 카페(http://cafe.naver.com/readingtc)를 방문해 보세요. 이미 수만 명의 회원들이 모여서 '북클럽'을 통해 함께 원서를 읽고 있습니다. 13만 명이 넘는 회원들이 단순히 함께 원서를 읽는 것뿐만 아니라, 위에서 언급한 다양한 방식으로 원서를 활용하여 영어 실력을 실질적으로 향상시키고 있습니다. 여러분도 스피드 리딩 카페를 방문해 보신다면 많은 자극과 도움을 받으실 수 있을 것입니다.

원서 읽기 습관을 길러 보세요!

일상에서 영어를 한마디도 쓰지 않는 비영어권 국가에서 살고 있는 우리가 영어 환경에 가장 쉽고, 편하고, 부담 없이 노출되는 방법은 바로 '영어원서 읽기'입니다. 언제 어디서든 원서를 붙잡고 읽기만 하면 곧바로 영어를 접하는 환경이 만들어지기 때문이지요. 하루에 20분씩만 꾸준히 읽는다면, 1년에 무려 120시간 동안 영어에 노출될 수 있습니다. 이런 이유 때문에 영어 교육 전문가들이 영어원서 읽기를 추천하는 것이지요.

영어원서를 꾸준히 읽어 보세요. '원서 읽기 습관'을 만들어 보세요! 이렇게 영어를 접하는 시간이 늘어나면, 영어 실력도 당연히 향상될 수밖에 없습니다. 아래 표에는 영어 수준별 추천 원서들이 있습니다. 하지만 이것은 절대적인 기준이 아니며, 학습자의 영어 수준과 관심 분야에 따라 개인적인 책 선정은 달라질 수 있습니다. 이 책은 Level 3에 해당합니다. 이 책의 완독 경험을 기준으로 삼아 적절한 책을 골라 꾸준히 읽어 보세요.

영어 수준별 추천 원서 목록

리딩 레벨	영어 수준	원서 목록
Level 1	유치원생 초등학생	「The Zack Files」 시리즈, 「Magic Tree House」 시리즈, 「Junie B. Jones」 시리즈, 「Horrid Henry」 시리즈, 로알드 달 단편들 (「The Giraffe and the Pelly and Me」, 「Esio Trot」, 「The Enormous Crocodile」, 「The Magic Finger」, 「Fantastic Mr. Fox」 등)
Level 2	초 · 중학생	「Spiderwick Chronicles」 시리즈, 쉬운 뉴베리 수상작들 (「Sarah, Plain and Tall」, 「The Hundred Dresses」 등), 앤드류 클레먼츠 단편들 (「Frindle」, 「The School Story」 등), 짧고 간단한 자기계발서 (「Who Moved My Cheese?」, 「The Present」 등)
Level 3	중 · 고등학생	「Wayside School」 시리즈, 「A Series of Unfortunate Events」 시리즈, 중간 수준의 뉴베리 수상작들 (「Number the Stars」, 「Charlotte's Web」 등), 로알드 달 장편들 (「Charlie and the Chocolate Factory」, 「Matilda」 등)
Level 4	대학생	「Harry Potter」 시리즈 중 1~3권, 「Percy Jackson」 시리즈, 「The Chronicles of Narnia」 시리즈, 「The Alchemist」, 어려운 수준의 뉴베리 수상작들 (「Holes」, 「The Giver」 등)
Level 5	이전 레벨의 원서 완독 유경험자	「Harry Potter」 시리즈 중 4~7권, 「Shopaholic」 시리즈, 「His Dark Materials」 시리즈, 「The Devil Wears Prada」, 「The Curious Incident of the Dog in the Night-Time」, 「Tuesdays With Morrie」 등

*참고 자료: Renaissance Learning, ReadingTown USA, Slyvan Learning Center

「영화로 읽는 영어원서」로 원서 읽기 습관을 만들어 보세요!

『주토피아』를 재미있게 읽은 독자라면 「영화로 읽는 영어원서」 시리즈를 꾸준히 읽어 보시길 추천해 드립니다. 「영화로 읽는 영어원서」 시리즈는 유명 영화를 기반으로 한 소설판 영어원서로 보다 쉽고 부담 없이 원서 읽기를 시작할 수 있도록 도와주고, 오디오북을 기본적으로 포함해 원서의 활용 범위를 넓힌 책입니다.

『엔칸토: 마법의 세계』, 『소울』, 『겨울왕국』, 『인사이드 아웃』, 『모아나』, 『코코』 등 출간하는 책마다 독자들의 큰 사랑을 받으며 어학 분야의 베스트셀러를 기록했고, 학원과 학교에서도 꾸준히 교재로 채택되는 등 영어 학습자들에게도 좋은 반응을 얻고 있습니다. (전국 소재 중·고교 방과 후 보충 교재 채택, 전국 영어 학원 정·부교재 채택, 초등학교 영어원서 읽기 대회 교재 채택 등)

CHAPTERS 1 & 2

1. D "Back then, the world was divided in two: vicious predator or meek prey." Two cardboard boxes dropped down from the ceiling. The first, labeled VICIOUS PREDATOR in crayon, landed on top of the jaguar, and the second, labeled MEEK PREY, landed on Judy. The boxes settled on their shoulders so their heads, arms, and legs stuck out. "But over time, we evolved and moved beyond our primitive, savage ways."

2. C "But just two hundred and eleven miles away stands the great city of . . . ZOOTOPIA! Where our ancestors first joined together in peace. And declared that Anyone Can Be Anything! Thank you and good night!"

3. D "Or . . . heck, you wanna talk about making the world a better place—no better way to do it than becoming a carrot farmer," said Stu.

4. B "Cry, little baby bunny. Cry, cry—" Gideon taunted. *Bam!* Before Gideon could say another word, Judy kicked him in the face with her hind legs, knocking him down. But he sprang right back up, and he was mad. "Oh, you don't know when to quit, do you?" Gideon said, unsheathing his claws like a fist of knives.

5. A Judy slapped her police hat back on top of her head, and there was a look of determination in her eye. "Well, he was right about one thing: I don't know when to quit."

CHAPTERS 3 & 4

1. C In the final weeks of training, Judy used her bunny skills, like her strong legs and her great hearing, to help prove her worth. She sailed through the physical obstacles and at times even passed the other cadets. Once, she knocked down a male rhino ten times her size during a final sparring session!

2. A "We're real proud of you, Judy," said Bonnie. "Yeah. Scared, too," said Stu. "Really, it's a proud-scared combo. I mean, Zootopia. It's so far away and such a big city."

3. D "Come on. When is there not a need for a fox Taser?" asked Stu. "Okay, I will take this to make you stop talking," said Judy. She grabbed the pink can of fox repellent as the train approached.

4. B She looked down at her phone and checked her maps app to figure out which way to go. When she found her apartment building, the landlady, Dharma, an armadillo, led her to a little apartment.

5. B "Greasy walls . . . rickety bed . . . ," said Judy. Then loud voices came from the other side of the wall: "Shut up!" "You shut up!" "No! You shut up!" "Crazy neighbors." Judy flopped onto the bed with a big smile. "I *love* it!"

CHAPTERS 5 & 6

1. A "O-M goodness!" he said. "They really did hire a bunny. What! I gotta tell you; you are even cuter than I thought you'd be." Judy winced. "Oh, uh, I'm sure you didn't know, but for us rabbits . . . the word 'cute' is a—it's a little—" "Oh! I am so sorry. *Me,* Benjamin Clawhauser, the guy everyone thinks is just a flabby, donut-loving cop, stereotyping *you* . . . ," he said apologetically.

2. B "Number two: there are some new recruits with us I should introduce. But I'm not going to, because I don't care."

3. A Bogo moved toward a map. "Finally, we have fourteen missing mammal cases," he said, gesturing to the pushpin-covered map. "FOURTEEN CASES. Now, that's more than we've ever had, and City Hall is right up my tail to solve them. This is priority one. Assignments!"

4. A When Judy noticed the little toddler clinging to the fox's leg, she felt awful for jumping to conclusions. "I'm such a . . . ," Judy muttered to herself as she turned to leave.

5. C The fox turned to Judy. "Thank you so much. Thank you." He dug through his pockets before stopping in disbelief. "Are you kidding me? I don't have my wallet. I'm sorry, pal, worst birthday ever." The fox leaned down to give the toddler a kiss, then turned to Judy. "Thanks anyway." Judy slapped some cash on the counter. "Keep the change," she said.

CHAPTERS 7 & 8

1. D Nick's son was using his little paws to make molds in the snow, which Nick then put sticks in. Then the two poured the juice from the melted Jumbo-pop into the molds to create dozens of smaller pops! Judy looked on, scandalized. She couldn't believe it! Judy followed them again, this time to Savanna Central, where they set up a stand and sold "pawpsicles" at marked-up prices to lemmings. "Pawpsicles! Get your pawpsicles!" barked Nick.

2. B She continued to follow Nick and Finnick to Little Rodentia, where Nick plopped down the bundle of used sticks in front of a mouse construction worker and shouted, "Lumber delivery!"

3. C "Hey," she said, hurrying to catch up as Nick strolled along. "All right, slick Nick, you're under arrest." "Really, for what?" "Gee, I don't know. How about selling food without a permit, transporting undeclared commerce across borough lines, false advertising—"

4. C "All right, look, everyone comes to Zootopia thinking they can be anything they want. Well, you can't. You can only be what you are." He pointed to himself. "Sly fox." Then he pointed to her. "Dumb bunny."

5. A Bonnie peered into the screen trying to see what Stu was so excited about. "Oh my sweet heaven! Judy, are you a meter maid?" Judy had forgotten she was still wearing her vest and that her hat was on the chair. She tried to backpedal. "What? Oh, this? No. It's just a temporary—" "It's the safest job on the force!" exclaimed Bonnie happily.

CHAPTERS 9 & 10

1. B Then the weasel ducked into the tiny community of Little Rodentia. The large cops, who had joined in the chase, couldn't fit through the gate, but Judy was small enough to follow the weasel in. … Judy watched the weasel jump off the top of a mouse building, tipping it over. She struggled to protect each and every building the weasel knocked into. Then he leapt on top of a moving mouse train! "Bon voyage, flatfoot!" said the weasel with a chuckle, riding the train away. But Judy wasn't about to give up. She ran even faster, until she was able to push him off the train. Rodents screamed and ran as Judy and the weasel came barreling through their midst. … A second before it crushed the shrew, Judy moved in front of the donut and caught it in her arms.

2. C Out of the corner of her eye, Judy noticed that the weasel was about to get away. She threw the giant donut over his head and around his body, trapping him inside. The weasel was stuck!

3. B Bogo forced a smile and closed the door. He turned to Judy, even angrier than before. "I will give you forty-eight hours," he said. "YES!" cried Judy. "That's two days to find Emmitt Otterton."

4. A She grabbed Clawhauser's empty soda bottle. She looked through it, using the glass at the bottom to magnify the image. Now she could see Mr. Otterton holding a frozen treat. She examined it and said thoughtfully, "Pawpsicle."

5. B "Nicholas Wilde, you are under arrest," Judy said. Nick smiled, amused. "For what?

"Felony tax evasion," she replied.

CHAPTERS 11 & 12

1. **A** Judy approached Yax. "Hello! My name is—" "Oh, you know, I'm gonna hit the pause button right there. We are all good on Bunny Scout Cookies," said Yax, who talked slowly, almost as if he wasn't quite there.

2. **C** "Thank you so much," said Judy. "That would be a big—" Yax came around from behind the counter, and Judy was unable to complete her sentence when she saw what he was—or wasn't—wearing. "You are naked!" "Huh? Oh, for sure, we're a Naturalist Club," said Yax nonchalantly.

3. **A** "He was here a couple Wednesdays ago. 'Member?" Yax prompted Nanga. But the elephant just shook her head. "Nope." "Yeah," Yax continued. "He was wearing a green cable-knit sweater-vest and a new pair of corduroy slacks. Oh, and a paisley tie, sweet Windsor knot, real tight. Remember that, Nanga?" Judy couldn't believe her luck. Yax was a gold mine! She scrambled to write everything down.

4. **C** "No, not forever. I have"—Judy paused as she checked her phone—"thirty-six hours left to solve this case. Can you run the plate or not?" Nick stared at Judy, and then slowly grinned. "I just remembered, I have a pal at the DMV."

5. **B** "They're all sloths!" Judy exclaimed, noticing the employees. Nick smiled. "You said this was going to be quick!" "What? Are you saying that because he's a sloth, he can't be fast?" Nick said innocently. "I thought in Zootopia anyone could be anything."

CHAPTERS 13 & 14

1. **D** "The thing is, " Judy said, "you don't need a warrant if you have probable cause. And I'm pretty sure I saw a shifty lowlife climbing the fence, so you're helping plenty. Come on," she said, heading off as she whistled a merry tune.

2. **B** Judy spotted a wallet on the floor and picked it up. She opened it to find Mr. Otterton's driver's license and business cards for his floral shop. "This is him! Emmitt Otterton. He was definitely here. What do you think happened?"

3. **C** "Why? Whose car is it?" she asked. Nick rushed around the limo, nervously trying to put everything back the way they found it. "The most dangerous crime boss in Tundratown.

They call him Mr. Big, and *he* does *not* like me, so we've gotta go!"

4. B "What did you do to make Mr. Big so mad at you?" Judy asked Nick. "I, uh, may or may not have sold him a very expensive wool rug . . . that was made from the fur of a . . . skunk's butt," Nick said quietly.

5. A Nick and Judy screamed. "Wait. WAIT!" Fru Fru shouted. "I know her. She's the bunny who saved my life yesterday. From that giant donut."

CHAPTERS 15 & 16

1. A "Otterton is my florist," said Mr. Big. "He's like a part of the family. He had something important he wanted to discuss. That's why I sent that car to pick him up. But he never arrived."

2. B "Because he was attacked," said Judy. "No . . . *he* attacked," Mr. Big explained. "He went crazy. Ripped up the car, scared my driver half to death, and disappeared into the night."

3. D Finally, the door slowly creaked open, just a crack. "You should be asking . . . what happened to *me*," said a voice from inside. The chain lock prevented the door from opening all the way. Through the space, they could see that Manchas was a big jaguar and he had been badly beaten, with bruises, scratches, and a black eye.

4. C Manchas described the scene, sounding haunted. Like he was reliving it. "He was an *animal*, down on all fours. He was a savage. There was no warning, just kept yelling about the 'night howlers, the night howlers,' over and over."

5. B Nick screamed as Manchas charged at him full speed. A split second before he reached Nick—*clank!* Manchas was yanked back by a handcuff on his back paw. Judy had cuffed him to a metal post! Nick couldn't believe it—Judy had saved his life.

CHAPTERS 17 & 18

1. B Judy stared at Nick. She couldn't believe he was sticking up for her. Bogo stood silently. "Here's the thing, Chief. You gave her forty eight hours, so technically we still have ten left to find our Mr. Otterton . . . and that's exactly what we are gonna do. So if you'll excuse us . . . we have a very big lead to follow and a case to crack. Good day."

2. C "I learned two things that day," said Nick, lost in the terrible memory. "One, I was

never going to let anyone see that they got to me." "And two?" Judy prodded. "If the world's only gonna see a fox as shifty and untrustworthy, there's no point trying to be anything else."

3. A "Wait! The Jam Cams!" said Nick urgently. "Seriously, it's okay," said Judy. "N-no, shh-shush! There are traffic cameras everywhere. All over the canopy. Whatever happened to that jaguar—" "The traffic cameras would have caught it!" said Judy, excitedly, suddenly realizing what Nick meant.

4. B "This is so exciting, actually. Well, you know, I never get to do anything this important," said Bellwether.

5. A "Howlers. Night howlers," said Judy. "That's what Manchas was afraid of—wolves! The wolves are the night howlers. If they took Manchas—" "I bet they took Otterton, too," said Nick.

CHAPTER 19 &20

1. A It was Judy, hidden beneath the cliffs! Hearing the sound, the wolf couldn't help but howl back. Another guard approached and said sharply, "Quit it, Gary. You're gonna start a howl." "I didn't start it. Oooooooooo!" said Gary. Unable to control it, the other guard howled back. Soon more and more wolves joined in, howling away. Judy whispered to Nick, "Come on!" They used the distraction to jump the fence and sneak by the guards.

2. B "Mayor Lionheart, please," said the doctor. "We're doing everything we can." "Oh, I don't think you are," said Lionheart. "Because I got a dozen and a half animals here who've gone off-the-freaking-rails crazy, and you can't tell me why. I'd call that *awfully* far from *doing everything.*"

3. C "Biology, Doctor? Spare me." "We both know what they all have in common. We can't keep it a secret. We need to come forward," the doctor said. Lionheart snarled and turned on the doctor. "What do you think will happen if the press gets ahold of this?"

4. D "Mayor Lionheart, you are under arrest for the kidnapping and false imprisonment of innocent citizens," Judy said as she cuffed him.

5. A "Clearly there's a biological component," he said sarcastically, repeating her words. "These predators may be reverting back to their primitive savage ways." He looked at her incredulously. "Are you serious?" "I just stated the facts of the case," said Judy. "I mean, it's not like a bunny could go savage."

CHAPTER 21 & 22

1. B After the press conference, a wedge was driven between the animals of Zootopia, and everyone was talking about it. There were conflicts and protests. The animals began to treat one another differently.

2. D "Oh, they thought it would be better if a *predator* such as myself wasn't the first face you see when you walk into the ZPD. So they're moving me to Records downstairs. By the boiler," he said.

3. C "With all due respect, sir, a good cop is supposed to serve and protect—help the city, not tear it apart," said Judy. She took off her badge and handed it to Bogo. "I don't deserve this badge."

4. D "He's our partner! And we'd never have considered it had you not opened our minds," said Bonnie. "That's right," said Stu. "Gid's turned into one of the top pastry chefs in the triboroughs."

5. C "Now, there's a four-dollar word, Mr. H. My family always just called them night howlers," said Gideon. Judy's ears pricked up. "What did you say?" she asked. Stu gestured to the flowers growing on the edge of the crops. "Oh, Gid's talking about those flowers, Judy. I use them to keep bugs off the produce. But I don't like the little ones going near them on account of your Uncle Terry." "Yeah, Terry ate one whole when we were kids and went completely nuts," said Bonnie. "He bit the dickens out of your mother," added Stu. "A bunny can go savage . . . ," said Judy, putting the pieces together.

CHAPTERS 23 & 24

1. C "Night howlers aren't wolves. They're toxic flowers. I think someone is targeting predators on purpose and making them go savage."

2. B "Wait, listen! I know you'll never forgive me. And I don't blame you. I wouldn't forgive me, either. I was ignorant and irresponsible and small-minded. But predators shouldn't suffer because of my mistakes. I have to fix this, but I can't do it without you."

3. D Judy and Nick found Weaselton standing on a street corner, selling random junk. "Anything you need . . . I got it," he called. "All your favorite movies! I got movies that haven't even been released yet!" In front of him were knockoff movies like *Wreck-It Rhino, Wrangled,* and *Pig Hero 6.*

4. A "We both know those weren't moldy onions I caught you stealing," said Judy. "What were you going to do with those night howlers, Wezzleton?"

5. C "Ice this weasel," Mr. Big ordered. "Wait! Stop! I'll talk!" screamed Weaselton. "I stole them night howlers because I could sell them for a lot of dough."

CHAPTERS 25 & 26

1. C Judy and Nick shared a look. It was suddenly clear. The map contained the images of all the missing animals. The ram must have hit them with the serum from the night howlers, turning them all savage.

2. B "We need to get this evidence to the ZPD," said Judy. "Okay. Got it," said Nick, picking up the case. "No. All of it," said Judy, smiling.

3. C Judy turned to go, but the sheep blocked their way. Why wouldn't Bellwether let them leave? All of a sudden, it became crystal clear to Judy. Bellwether was the one behind this from the very beginning! That was why she had known where they would be.

4. D "So that's it? Prey fears predator, and you stay in power?" asked Judy. "Pretty much," said Bellwether. "It won't work," said Judy. "Fear always works," said Bellwether. "And I'll dart every predator in Zootopia to keep it that way."

5. C Nick held up the ball of serum, then gestured to the gun. "Yeah," he said. "Oh, are you looking for the serum? Well, it's right here." "What you've got in the weapon there—those are blueberries. From my family's farm," said Judy.

CHAPTERS 27 & 28

1. B "Did I falsely imprison those animals? Well, yes. Yes, I did. Classic 'doing the wrong thing for the right reason' scenario. Know what I mean, Kitty?"

2. A Back in the studio, the newscaster continued. "In related news, doctors say the night howler antivenom is proving effective in rehabilitating all of the victims." When Mr. Otterton awoke inside the hospital, his wife was hugging him tightly. Judy was there, watching and smiling.

3. C Judy and Nick took their seats among the other cops in the bullpen. Bogo stood up at the front, calling order. "We have some new recruits with us this morning," said Bogo. "Including our first fox. But . . . who cares?"

4. C "Shut your mouth, Wilde," said Bogo, then began calling out assignments. When he finally got to Judy and Nick, they waited eagerly. "Hopps, Wilde . . . Skunk Pride Parade. Dismissed."

5. D "Sly bunny," said Nick, wiping his face. "Dumb fox." "Come on, you know I love you," said Nick. "Do I know that? Yes. Yes, I do."

주토피아(ZOOTOPIA)

1판 1쇄 2016년 3월 14일
1판 13쇄 2024년 4월 8일

지은이 Suzanne Francis
기획 김승규
책임편집 정소이 김보경
콘텐츠제작및감수 롱테일 교육 연구소
번역 배서영
마케팅 두잉글 사업 본부

펴낸이 이수영
펴낸곳 롱테일북스
출판등록 제2015-000191호
주소 04033 서울특별시 마포구 양화로 113, 3층(서교동, 순흥빌딩)
전자메일 help@ltinc.net

ISBN 979-11-86701-12-6 14740